"I have now come to understand the extraordinary importance of leading an integral life. That is, of allowing myself to first notice, then to blend, all the aspects of who I am—those that I and others called 'positive' and those that I and others have called 'negative'—into a grander Whole.

"Through this process I have made friends with myself at last. But, oh, how long it took to get there! And how much shorter the process would have been had I been exposed to the deep insights and the wonderful wisdom in this book.

"Read this book carefully. Read it once, and read it once again. Then read it a third time for good measure. I dare you."

—From the foreword by Neale Donald Walsch,
author of *Conversations with God*

"The path to enlightenment includes not only the search for the divine but also the total acceptance of the shadow self. In this profound book, Debbie Ford systematically outlines the steps to wholeness and transformation."

—Deepak Chopra, M.D.,
author of *The Seven Spiritual Laws of Success*

"Through her own inner work and inner journey, Debbie Ford has developed a powerful understanding of how life mirrors to us the way we relate to ourselves. This book is an invitation, backed up by clear, simple methods, to embark on the great work of learning to embrace all that we are."

—John Welwood,
author of *Love and Awakening*

DEBBIE FORD

RIVERHEAD BOOKS

NEW YORK

THE DARK SIDE OF
THE LIGHT CHASERS

RECLAIMING YOUR

POWER, CREATIVITY,

BRILLIANCE, AND

DREAMS

Most Riverhead Books are available at special quantity discounts for bulk pur-
chases for sales promotions, premiums, fund-raising or educational use. Special
books, or book excerpts, can also be created to fit specific needs.

For details, write: Special Markets, The Berkley Publishing Group, 375 Hudson
Street, New York, New York 10014.

RIVERHEAD BOOKS
Published by The Berkley Publishing Group
A division of Penguin Putnam Inc.
375 Hudson Street
New York, New York 10014

First Riverhead hardcover edition: May 1998
First Riverhead trade paperback edition: June 1999
Riverhead trade paperback ISBN: 1-57322-735-8

The Penguin Putnam Inc. World Wide Web site address is
http://www.penguinputnam.com

The Library of Congress has catalogued the Riverhead hardcover edition as follows:

Ford, Debbie.
The dark side of the light chasers : reclaiming your
power, creativity, brilliance, and dreams /
by Debbie Ford.
p.   cm.
ISBN 1-57322-096-5
1. Shadow (Psychoanalysis).   2. Self-realization.
I. Title.
BF175.5.S55F67   1998   98-9563 CIP

Printed in the United States of America

10   9

ACKNOWLEDGMENTS

From the deepest place in my heart, I express my love and gratitude to everyone who has loved and supported me in the birth of this book.

To my sister, the brilliant and beautiful Arielle Ford, for being my best friend, biggest fan, and manager, and for sharing my vision for health and wholeness.

To Peter Guzzardi, who gave me the confidence to write this book, for always guiding me back to my message while sharing his love and insights.

To Deepak Chopra for welcoming me into his spiritual family and for graciously opening the door to endless possibilities and guiding me in developing my work.

To Rita Chopra for her continuous love and generosity.

To Dr. David Simon for being a kindred spirit and sharing his fabulous insights with me.

To Neale Donald Walsch for supporting me in bringing my work out into the world.

To Stephen Samuels, my friend and teacher, who gave me

back my youth and my aliveness. Thank you for all the hours you spent making me look deeper and for helping me in finishing this book.

To my beloved father in heaven, Judge Harvey Ford, for honoring and respecting my dreams.

To my brother, Michael Ford, for always believing in me.

To my second father, Dr. Howard Fuerst, for being a great model for all of us who want to heal and transform our lives.

To Gramma Ada for always accepting me and supporting me in finishing my education.

To my family for their unconditional love: Aunt Pearl; Aunt Laura; Uncle Sandy; Uncle Stanley; Judy Ford; Anne Ford; Ashley, Eve, Sarah, and Tyler Logan Ford; Bernice Bressler, and Marty Bressler.

To Brian Hilliard for joining my family and participating in my life and career.

To Dan Bressler for being a fantastic father to our son, Beau, and for supporting me while I wrote this book.

To Susan Petersen for her insight and commitment to this book.

To Wendy Carlton for her commitment to excellence and for being the best editor anyone could ask for. To Jennifer Repo, Rachel Knowles, and the magnificent staff at Putnam.

To my best friends: Rachel Levy for encouraging and loving me through this enormous project, and for working nonstop to produce *The Shadow Process* in Miami. Danielle Dorman for listening to me for countless hours and supporting me to no end.

And to their saintly husbands, Henry Levy and Patrick Dorman, for understanding the demands of true friendship.

To Jeremiah Abrams for being a loving teacher and friend.

To Nan Johnson, Chelsea Peters, and the entire staff of the Chopra Center for Well Being.

To Landmark Education Corporation, the Hoffman Quadrinity Process, and JFK University for educating and training me. To my teachers Susanne West, Dr. Barry Martin, and Sandra Delay, who deeply touched my life.

To Rich Petrick, thanks for moving me out west and leading me to a new realm of reality. To my friends in San Francisco: Sherill Edwards, Curt Hill, Nancy Kleinman, Joan Bordeaux, and Susan August. And to all the many participants in my Oakland seminars, thank you for training me.

To the thousands of people who have attended my lectures and courses, who have given themselves so generously, and who have shared their intimate lives with me. Without them this book would not have been possible.

To my dear friend Brent BecVar for all his enthusiasm and love.

Thank you to all my friends who helped me through my toughest times: Luba Bozanich, Amy Karen, Joyce Ostin, Michael Mindich, Robert Lee, Howard Schwartz, Bill Spinoza, Barbara Marks, Samantha Hudson, Jan Smith, Joni Lang, Carol Sontag, Sue Campbell, Alys Marks, and Julie and Jerry Brown.

To Monroe Zalkin for always believing in me. To Don Soffer, who taught me what it means to have a generous heart. To my dear friend Olaf Halvorssen, whose faith and persistence always inspire me. To Fred Greene, who taught me the meaning of compassion.

To all my friends for being there during the brightest moments and the darkest hours: Loree and Cliff Edwards, Francis Warner, Sarah McClain, Vivian Glyck, Patty Eddy, Kimberly Wise, Michael Clark, Jennifer Mercurio, Peter Lawrence, Carla Picardi, Terri Garcia, Margaret Bhola, Sherri Davis, Becky Hansen, Dennis Schmucker, Elyse Santoro, Vera Pacillo, Alisha Starr, and Shelly Star. To Midge McDonald and Marcella Flekalova for loving and nurturing my body and soul.

To my soul sister Adriana Nienow for her extraordinary love and courage.

To my Public Relations angels, Katherine Kellmeyer and Laura Clark, the staff at the fabulous Ford Group.

To all those I might have neglected to mention, you are not forgotten. Thank you for touching my heart and touching my life.

To Anthony Benson, my new old friend, for being there in the eleventh hour.

To my dear friend Randy Thomas who graciously shares her knowledge and love with me.

To Geeta Singh and The Talent Exchange for doing such a great job setting up and watching over my career.

To Donna Karen for her courage and willingness to share herself and her heart. Thank you for all you have done for me.

To Donna's incredible staff who has been there to support me in my mission and image, Susan Gardner, Jennifer Wasserman, and Julie Priddle. And Katherine Boyd for the magnificent interview.

To Marianne Williamson, John Welwood, Dean Ornish, M.D., Harold Bloomfield, M.D., and Sirah Vettese, Ph.D., for their commitment to bringing health and healing to our planet, for supporting my work, and being great role models.

To my dear friends Dianne and Alan Collins for their amazing coaching and for their brilliant program, Quantum Think, Audio-Coach.

To my beautiful son, Beau Bressler, for teaching me about unconditional love and for opening my heart wider than I could ever imagine. And to his wonderful nanny, Roberta Morales, who took such special care of us while I wrote.

I have been blessed by the wisdom of the universe. It comes to me every time I close my eyes and listen. Thank you, God, for allowing me to express this information. Thank you for guiding me and protecting me. From the deepest place in my heart, I love you.

This book is dedicated to

my beautiful mother, Sheila Fuerst.

Thank you for giving me the gift of life and for being my mom.

CONTENTS

Shadow work has been around for the longest time. It is the very essence of the religious impulse, where traditionally we have sought a balance between the light and dark. Remember Lucifer, who at one time was the brightest of the angels? His fall is the temptation we all meet. We are continually called upon to be morally aware lest we come under the influence of the dark side.

I was recently reminded of the perennial nature of shadow work by an audience member in Minneapolis, who stood up following a talk I had just given on the shadow, and asked, "Aren't you just pouring old wine into new bottles?"

"Well, yes," I said, somewhat surprised that he had made this connection. "The dark side has been a part of all of our religious traditions. But we are always in need of new containers and new language that is contemporaneous with the human predicament. Yes, that's right," I repeated, "shadow work is old wine."

This questioner reminded me of the many clients who have confronted shadow in my consulting room over the years. Each generation needs new ways to speak of the phenomenon of shadow, both the positive and negative shadow. Dark doesn't mean only negative, it refers to something that is out of the light of our conscious awareness. The initial phase of therapeutic counsel is a confessional, and much like the venerable Catholic institution of confession, we hear of failure and misdeeds, of how someone has arrived at a sorry circumstance, or has not been able to realize his or her positive potential. We are challenged to give reality and meaning to what may be working through a client, to help them become more aware of the denied parts of themselves. The greatest sin may be the unlived life.

In that spontaneous moment in Minnesota I was also reminded of what the eminent Swiss psychologist C. G. Jung wrote in his 1937 book, *Psychology and Religion,* that "to gain an understanding of religious matters, probably all that is left us today is the psychological approach. That is why I take these thought-forms that have become historically fixed, try to melt them down again, and pour them into molds of immediate experience."

The concept of the shadow is such a mold. It is a way to symbolize in language the unowned side of personality and give it reality, a means to get hold of and talk about our unknown parts. Shadow refers to that portion of us that is constantly shifting and changing in the light of our ego consciousness, those aspects of self that we fail to bring fully to responsible awareness. As individuals and as members of a specific culture, we are continually selecting and editing experience, creating an ego-based ideal of self and world. The more we seek the light, the denser the Shadow becomes.

We know the shadow by many names: dark side, alter ego, lower self, the other, the double, the dark twin, disowned self, repressed self, id. We speak of meeting our demons, wrestling with the devil (the devil made me do it), a descent to the underworld, a dark night of the soul, a midlife crisis.

Shadow begins with the earliest emancipation of an "I" from the great unity consciousness from which we all have come. Shadow-making runs parallel to ego development. What doesn't fit our developing ego-ideal—our idealized sense of self, individualistically reinforced by family and culture—becomes shadow. Poet and author Robert Bly calls the shadow the "long bag we drag behind us." "We spend our life until we're twenty deciding what parts of ourselves to put in the bag," Bly says, "and we spend the rest of our lives trying to get them out again."

"Would you rather be whole or good?" asked Jung, the person who coined the poetic term shadow and molded the concept for our era. Jung paid special attention to the work of integrating the shadow, suggesting that it was an initiation to psychological life— the apprentice-piece, he called it—an essential awareness for our self-realization. "Realization of the shadow is an eminently practical problem," he said, "which should not be twisted into an intellectual activity, for it has far more the meaning of a suffering and a passion that implicate the whole person."

Shadow work, as Debbie Ford so clearly describes it in this book, refers to an ongoing process of depolarizing and balancing, of healing the split between our conscious sense of self and all else we are or might be. Like the practice called the "Middle Way" in Buddhism, shadow integration gives us a unifying awareness that allows us to reduce the shadow's inhibiting or destructive potentials, releasing trapped life energies that may be caught in the pretenses and posturing required to conceal what we can't accept about ourselves. This work has benefits that reach far beyond the personal and can work for the greatest collective good. If we are balancing the tensions that arise in our own garden, those effects will move out into all the fields of the earth.

We should not take for granted a book about shadow. It is a hard-won gift, a treasure lore wrested from the gods, often at great heroic sacrifice. A book about the shadow is not just for our minds, but is best understood by our hearts and our imaginations.

The Dark Side of the Light Chasers is old wine in new bottles. It has retained the satisfying taste and bouquet. The package is contemporary, a shadow integration process suitable for our times. We should take Debbie Ford's advice and, here at the outset, sac-rilize our own shadow work as an offering to the highest in us: to love, to compassion, to the heart's task. As the wise spirit of the *I Ching,* or *Book of Changes,* reminds us:

It is only when we have the courage
to face things exactly as they are,
without any self-deception or illusion,
that a light will develop out of events,
by which the path to success
may be recognized.

I Ching,
Hexagram 5, Hsü,
Waiting (Nourishment)

Jeremiah Abrams

I did not feel good about myself as a kid. In fact, there were times when I really hated being me. I thought I was the only one in the world who was so inept, so unable to make friends, and so ridiculed by the boyhood fraternity which I desperately—and fruitlessly—sought to join.

Not much changed when I became a young adult. Oh, I thought I was going to strike out on a new course. I even moved to a new city, where nobody knew me. Where no one would know about my childhood tendency to brag a lot as a compensation for my lack of self-regard. No one would have seen what the adults of my childhood called my "flightiness." And no one would know about my habit of "coming on too strong," filling the room with my presence to the point where no one else felt they had any space in which to show up. My social ineptitudes would never be discovered.

Well, I found that moving didn't help. I had taken myself with me.

Then one day I found myself in a personal growth retreat presented by the staff development department where I was employed. The retreat facilitator said something I will never forget.

"All of your so-called faults, all the things which you don't like about yourself are your greatest assets," she said. "They are simply overamplified. The volume has been turned up a bit too much, that's all. Just turn down the volume a little. Soon, you—and everyone else—will see your weaknesses as your strengths, your 'negatives' as your 'positives.' They will become wonderful tools, ready to work for you rather than against you. All you have to do is learn to call on these personality traits in amounts that are appropriate to the moment. Judge how much of your wonderful qualities are needed, and don't give any more than that."

I felt as if I'd been struck by lightning. I'd never heard anything like this before. Still, I knew instinctively that it was truth. My bragging was nothing more than overamplified confidence. What people called "flighty" or "foolhardy" in my youth was nothing more than spontaneity and positive thinking, once again overamped. And my coming on so strong was just my leadership ability, my verbal dexterity, and my willingness to step to the line—all three notches too high.

I realized then that all of these aspects of my being were qualities for which I had also been praised at one time or another. No wonder I had been confused!

It was only then, when I looked at my "shadow side," and I saw clearly why others sometimes called these my "negative" behaviors, that I also saw the gift in each of them. All I had to do was use those behaviors differently. Not repress them. Not disown them. Simply use them differently.

I have now come to understand the extraordinary importance of leading an integral life. That is, of allowing myself to first notice, then to blend, all the aspects of who I am—those that I and others have called "positive" and those that I and others have called "negative"—into a grander Whole.

Through this process I have made friends with myself at last. But, oh, how long it took to get there! And how much shorter the process would have been had I been exposed to the deep insights and the wonderful wisdom in this book by Debbie Ford.

Read this book carefully. Read it once, and read it once again. Then read it a third time for good measure. And do the exercises it suggests. I dare you.

Double dare you.

But neither read the book nor do the exercises if you don't want your life to change. Put the book down right now. Stick it on the top shelf of your bookcase, where you'll never reach again. Or give it to a friend. Because it will very likely be impossible to experience this book without also experiencing shifts in your life.

I believe in living a life of utter visibility. That means complete transparency. Nothing hidden, nothing denied. Not even the part of myself that I didn't want to look at, much less acknowledge. If you agree with me that visibility is the key to authenticity, and that authenticity is the doorway to your True Self, you will thank Debbie Ford from the depth of your being for this book. For it will lead you right to that doorway, beyond which is found lasting joy, inner peace, and a place of self-love so vast, you will at last find the room to unconditionally love others.

And once that cycle begins, you will change not only your life, you will truly begin to change the world.

Neale Donald Walsch
Ashland, Oregon
March 1998

CHAPTER I

WORLD WITHOUT, WORLD WITHIN

Most of us set out on the path to personal growth because at some point the burden of our pain becomes too much to bear. *The Dark Side of the Light Chasers* is about unmasking that aspect of ourselves which destroys our relationships, kills our spirit, and keeps us from fulfilling our dreams. It is what the psychologist Carl Jung called the shadow. It contains all the parts of ourselves that we have tried to hide or deny. It contains those dark aspects that we believe are not acceptable to our family, friends, and most importantly, ourselves. The dark side is stuffed deeply within our consciousness, hidden from ourselves and others. The message we get from this hidden place is simple: there is something wrong with me. I'm not okay. I'm not lovable. I'm not deserving. I'm not worthy.

Many of us believe these messages. We believe that if we look closely enough at what lies deep within us, we will find something horrible. We resist looking long and hard for fear of discovering someone we can't live with. We fear ourselves. We fear every thought and feeling we have ever repressed. Many of us are so disconnected from this fear we can only see it by reflection. We project it onto the world, onto our families and friends, and onto strangers. Our fear is so deep that the only way we can deal with it is either to hide or deny it. We become great imposters who fool ourselves and others. We become so good at this we actually forget that we are wearing masks to hide our authentic selves. We believe we are the persons we see in the mirror. We believe we are our bodies and our minds. Even after years of failed relationships, careers, diets, and dreams, we continue to suppress these disturbing internal messages. We tell ourselves we're okay and that things will get better. We put blinders over our eyes and plugs in our ears to keep the internal stories we create alive. I'm not okay. I'm not lovable. I'm not deserving. I'm not worthy.

Instead of trying to suppress our shadows, we need to unconceal, own and embrace the very things we are most afraid of facing. By "own," I mean *acknowledge* that a quality belongs to you. "It is the shadow that holds the clues," says the spiritual teacher and author Lazaris. "The shadow also holds the secret of change, change that can affect you on a cellular level, change that can affect your very DNA." Our shadows hold the essence of who we are. They hold our most treasured gifts. By facing these aspects of ourselves, we become free to experience our glorious totality: the good and the bad, the dark and the light. It is by embracing all of who we are that we earn the freedom to choose what we do in this world. As long as we keep hiding, masquerading, and projecting what is inside us, we have no freedom to be and no freedom to choose.

Our shadows exist to teach us, guide us, and give us the blessing of our entire selves. They are resources for us to expose and explore. The feelings that we have suppressed are desperate to be integrated into ourselves. They are only harmful when they are re-pressed: then they can pop up at the least opportune times. Their sneak attacks will handicap you in the areas of your life that mean the most.

Your life will be transformed when you make peace with your shadow. The caterpillar will become a breathtakingly beautiful butterfly. You will no longer have to pretend to be someone you're not. You will no longer have to prove you're good enough. When you embrace your shadow you will no longer have to live in fear. Find the gifts of your shadow and you will finally revel in all the glory of your true self. Then you will have the freedom to create the life you have always desired.

Every human being is born with a healthy emotional system. We love and accept ourselves when we are born. We don't make judgments about which parts of ourselves are good and which parts are bad. We dwell in the fullness of our being, living in the moment, and expressing ourselves freely. As we grow older, we begin to learn from the people around us. They tell us how to act, when to eat, when to sleep, and we begin to make distinctions. We learn which behaviors bring us acceptance and which bring us re-jection. We learn if we get a prompt response or if our cries go unanswered. We learn to trust the people around us or to fear the people around us. We learn consistency or inconsistency. We learn which qualities are acceptable in our environment and which are not. All of this distracts us from living in the moment and keeps us from expressing ourselves freely.

We need to revisit the experience of our innocence that allows us to accept all of who we are at every moment. This is where we need to be in order to have a healthy, happy, complete human ex-istence. This is the path. In Neale Donald Walsch's book *Con-versations with God,* God says:

Perfect love is to feeling what perfect white is to color. Many think that white is the absence of color. It is not. It is the inclusion of all color. White is every other color that exists combined. So, too, is love not the absence of emotion (hatred, anger, lust, jealousy, covertness), but the summation of all feeling? It is the sum total. The aggregate amount. The everything.

Love is inclusive: it accepts the full range of human emotion—the emotions we hide, the emotions we fear. Jung once said, "I'd rather be whole than good." How many of us have sold ourselves out in order to be good, to be liked, to be accepted?

Most of us were raised to believe that people have good qualities and bad qualities. And in order to be accepted we had to get rid of our bad qualities, or at least hide them. This way of thinking happens when we begin to individuate, as we distinguish our fingers from the slats of our crib, and distinguish ourselves from our parents. But as we get older we realize an even greater truth—that spiritually we are all interconnected. We are all part of each other. From this point of view we need to ask whether there really are good parts and bad parts of us. Or are all parts necessary to make a whole? Because how can we know good without knowing bad? How can we know love without knowing hate? How can we know courage without knowing fear?

This holographic model of the universe provides us with a revolutionary view of the connection between the inner and the outer world. According to this theory, every piece of the universe, no matter how we slice it, contains the intelligence of the whole. We, as individual beings, are not isolated and random. Each of us is a microcosm that reflects and contains the macrocosm. "If this is true," says consciousness researcher Stanislav Grof, "then we each hold the potential for having direct and immediate experiential access to virtually every aspect of the universe, extending our capacities well beyond the reach of our senses." We all contain the imprint of the entire universe within ourselves. As Deepak Chopra puts it, "We are not in the world, but the world is within us." Each of us possess every existing human quality. There is nothing we can see or conceive that we are not, and the purpose of our journey is to restore ourselves to this wholeness.

The saintly and the cynical, the divine and the diabolical, the courageous and the cowardly: all these aspects lie dormant in us and will act out if they are not recognized and integrated into our psyches. Many of us are frightened of the light as well as the dark. Many of us are frightened to look within ourselves, and fear has us put up walls so thick we no longer remember who we really are.

The Dark Side of the Light Chasers is about working through those walls and taking down the barriers we've constructed and looking, maybe for the first time, at who we are and what we're doing here. This book will take you on a journey that will change the way you see yourself, others, and the world. It will lead you to open your heart and fill it with awe and compassion for your own humanity. The Persian poet Rumi said, "By God, when you see your beauty, you'll be the idol of yourself." In these pages, I offer a process for discovering the beauty of your authentic self.

Jung first gave us the term "shadow" to refer to those parts of our personality that have been rejected out of fear, ignorance, shame, or lack of love. His basic notion of the shadow was simple: "the shadow is the person you would rather not be." He believed that integrating the shadow would have a profound impact, enabling us to rediscover a deeper source of our own spiritual life.

"To do this," Jung said, "we are obliged to struggle with evil, confront the shadow, to integrate the devil. There is no other choice."

You must go into the dark in order to bring forth your light. When we suppress any feeling or impulse, we are also suppressing its polar opposite. If we deny our ugliness, we lessen our beauty. If we deny our fear, we minimize our courage. If we deny our greed, we also reduce our generosity. Our full magnitude is more than most of us can ever imagine. If you believe that we have the imprint of all humanity within us, as I do, then you must be capable of being the greatest person you ever admired, and at the same time capable of being the worst person you ever imagined. This book is about making peace with all these sometimes contradictory aspects of your self.

My friend Bill Spinoza, a seminar leader for Landmark Education, says, "What you can't *be* with won't let you *be*." You've got to learn how to give all of who you are permission to exist. If you want to be free you must be able "to be." This means we must stop judging ourselves. We must forgive ourselves for being human. We must forgive ourselves for being imperfect. Because when we judge ourselves we automatically judge others. And what we do to others, we also do to ourselves. The world is a mirror of our internal selves. When we can accept ourselves, and forgive ourselves, we automatically accept and forgive others. This was a hard lesson for me to learn.

Thirteen years ago I woke up on the cold marble floor of my bathroom. My body ached and my breath stank. It had been another night of parties and drugs and then, of course, being sick. When I stood up and looked in the mirror, I knew I couldn't go on this way. I was twenty-eight and still waiting for someone to come and make me okay. But that morning I realized that no one was coming. My mother wasn't coming, my father wasn't coming, and my prince on the big white horse wasn't coming. I was at a crossroads in my drug addiction. I knew that very soon I would have to choose between life and death. No one else could make this choice for me. No one else could take away my pain. No one could help me until I helped myself. The woman standing in the mirror shocked me. I realized I had no idea who she was. It was as if I were seeing her for the first time. Tired and scared, I reached for a phone and called for help.

My life changed drastically. That morning I made the decision to get well, no matter how long it would take. After finishing a twenty-eight-day treatment program I set out on an odyssey to heal myself inside and out. It seemed like an enormous task but I knew I had no choice. Five years and approximately $50,000 later, I was a different person. I had healed my addictions, changed my friends, and altered my values. But when I got quiet in my meditations, there were still parts of myself that were not okay with me, parts that I wanted to get rid of. My problem was that I still hated myself.

It seems unbelievable that for eleven years someone could go to group therapy, codependency treatment, and twelve-step meetings, visit hypnotists and acupuncturists, experience rebirth, jump off mountains, attend transformational seminars, Buddhist retreats, and Sufi retreats, read hundreds of books, listen to visualization and meditation tapes, and still hate part of who she is. All that time, all that money, and I knew my work was still not done.

Then finally, something clicked. I was at a Leadership Intensive seminar led by a woman named Jan Smith. In the middle of the seminar, I was standing up in front of the group speaking when suddenly Jan looked at me and said, "You're a bitch." My heart sank. How did she know? I knew I was a bitch, but I had been trying desperately to get rid of this part of myself. I had worked hard to be sweet and generous to compensate for this awful trait. Then, dispassionately, Jan asked me why I hated this part of myself. Feeling small and stupid, I told her it was the part of me that caused me the most shame. I said that being a bitch had only brought myself and others pain. Then Jan said: "What you don't own, owns you."

I could see how being a bitch owned me, I worried about it all the time, but I still didn't want to own it. "What is good about being a bitch?" she asked. As far as I could see there was nothing good about it. But then she said, "If you were building a house, and the contractors were running over budget and were three weeks late, do you think it would help to be a little bitchy?" Of course, I said yes. "When you need to return merchandise in your business, does it help to be a bitch at times?" Of course, I said yes. Jan asked me if I could see now that being a bitch at certain times was not only useful but a great quality to possess if you wanted to get things done in the world. Suddenly this part of myself—which I'd tried desperately to hide, deny, and suppress—was set free. My whole body felt different. It was as if I had just dropped a hundred-pound weight from around my neck. Jan had taken this aspect of myself and showed me that it was a gift, that it was not something to feel shameful about. If I allowed it to exist, I wouldn't have to act it out. I would be able to use it, instead of it using me.

After that day, my life was never the same. Another piece of the healing puzzle had fallen into place. "What you resist, persists." I had heard it so many times, but I never fully understood the depth of the statement. By resisting the "bitch" in myself, I had kept it locked into place. The minute I accepted it and saw its gift, I relaxed my resistance, and it became a nonissue for me. It became a natural healthy part of who I was. Now I don't ever have to be a bitch, but if it is appropriate, which in this world it sometimes is, I can use that quality to take care of myself.

This process seemed miraculous to me. So I made a list of all the parts of myself I didn't like, and worked on finding the gifts in them. As soon as I was able to see the positive and the negative value of each aspect of myself, I was able to drop my defensiveness and allow these parts to exist freely. It became clear that the process was not about getting rid of things we dislike in ourselves, but about finding the positive side of these aspects and integrating it into our lives.

This book is a guide for your journey. It contains the essential ideas from a course I developed over the years to help unconceal, own, and embrace your shadow. I'll begin by defining the shadow in detail and exploring its nature and its effects. Then I'll examine the essential shadow phenomenon, projection, whereby we deny crucial parts of ourselves by giving them away. After we consider a new paradigm for understanding our inner and outer life—the holographic model of the universe—we can begin taking action, applying what we have learned to unconceal the hidden faces of our dark side. We will then embark on the process of owning and taking responsibility for our shadow qualities, learning specific tools for embracing the shadow and discovering its gifts, as well as how to take back the power over parts of ourselves that we have given to others. Finally, we will explore the ways in which we can love and nourish ourselves and the practical tools to manifest our dreams and to create a life worth living.

Many of us have spent too much time chasing the light only to find more darkness. "One does not become enlightened by imagining figures of light," said Jung, "but by making the darkness conscious." *The Dark Side of the Light Chasers* will guide you on your way to unconcealing, owning, and embracing your shadow. It will give you the knowledge and the tools to bring forth that which lies within you. It will guide you in reclaiming your power, your creativity, your brilliance, and your dreams. It will open up your heart to yourself and others, and alter your relationship with the world forever.

CHAPTER 2

CHASING DOWN THE SHADOW

The shadow wears many faces: fearful, greedy, angry, vindictive, evil, selfish, manipulative, lazy, controlling, hostile, ugly, undeserving, cheap, weak, critical, judgmental . . . The list goes on and on. Our dark side acts as a storehouse for all these unacceptable aspects of ourselves—all the things we pretend not to be and all the aspects that embarrass us. These are the faces we don't want to show the world and the faces we don't want to show ourselves.

Everything we hate, resist, or disown about ourselves takes on a life of its own, undermining our feelings of worthiness. When we come face-to-face with our dark side our first instinct is to turn away, and our second is to bargain with it to leave us alone. Many of us have spent vast amounts of time and money in an effort to do just that. Ironically, it's these hidden aspects we've rejected that need the most attention. When we locked away those parts of ourselves we didn't like, unknowingly, we sealed away our most valuable treasures. These valuables are therefore hidden where we would least expect to find them. They are hidden in the dark.

These treasures try desperately to emerge, to come to our attention, but we are conditioned to push them back down. Like giant beach balls being held underwater, these aspects pop back up to the surface whenever we take the pressure off. By choosing not to allow parts of ourselves to exist, we are forced to expend huge amounts of psychic energy to keep them beneath the surface.

Poet and author Robert Bly describes the shadow as an invisible bag that each of us carries around on our backs. As we're growing up we put in the bag every aspect of ourselves that is not acceptable to our families and friends. Bly believes we spend the first few decades of our lives filling up our bags, and spend the rest of our lives trying to retrieve everything we put in our bag in an effort to lighten our burdens.

Most people are afraid to confront and embrace their darkness, but it is in that very darkness you will find the happiness and fulfillment you have been longing for. When you take the time to discover your whole self, you'll open the door to true enlightenment. One of the biggest pitfalls of the Information Age is the "I know that" syndrome. Knowing often prevents us from experiencing through our hearts. Shadow work is not intellectual; it's a journey from the head to the heart. Many on the path to self-improvement believe they have completed the process but are unwilling to see the truth about themselves. Most of us long to see the light, and to live in the beauty of our highest self, but we try to do this without integrating all of ourselves. We can't have the full experience of the light without knowing the dark. The dark side is the gatekeeper to true freedom. Each of us must be willing to continually explore and expose this aspect of self. Whether you like it or not, if you're human, you have a shadow. If you can't see it, just ask the people in your family, or the people you work with. They'll point it out to you. We think that our masks keep our inner selves hidden, but whatever we refuse to recognize about ourselves has a way of rearing its head and making itself known when we least expect it.

Embracing an aspect of yourself means loving it—allowing it to coexist with all your other aspects, not making it more or less than any other part of yourself. It is not enough to say, "I know I am controlling." We must see what controlling has to teach us, what gift it brings, and then we must be able to view it with awe and compassion.

We live under the impression that in order for something to be divine it has to be perfect. We are mistaken. In fact, the exact opposite is true. To be divine is to be whole and to be whole is to be everything: the positive and the negative, the good and the bad, the holy man and the devil. When we take the time to discover our shadow and its gifts we will understand what Jung meant by, "The gold is in the dark." Each of us needs to find that gold in order to reunite with our sacred self.

When I was growing up I was told there were two kinds of people in the world: good and bad. Like most children, I worked to show off my good qualities and tried hard to hide my bad ones. I desperately wanted to get rid of all those parts of myself that were unacceptable to my mother, father, sister, and brother. As I got older more people came into my life with all their opinions, and I realized there was even more of myself I had to hide.

At night I often lay awake trying to figure out why I was such a bad girl. How was it possible that I had been cursed with so many awful qualities? I worried about my sister and brother who also had many deficiencies to overcome—anytime one of us showed any shortcoming we would get in trouble. I was told that the people down the street in the county jail were there because they had qualities that got them in trouble. I wanted to make sure I would not end up looking through bars to see my family and friends. So early on I figured that the best way to be accepted was to hide these undesirable parts of myself, which sometimes meant lying. My dream was to be perfect in order to be loved. So when I didn't brush my teeth, I lied, and when I ate more than my share of cookies, I lied, and when I bit my sister, I lied, and by the time I was three or four I did not even realize I was lying because I had already started lying to myself.

I was told, don't be angry, don't be selfish, don't be mean, don't be greedy. *Don't be* was the message I internalized. I started to believe I was a bad person because sometimes I was mean and sometimes I got angry and sometimes I wanted all the cookies. I believed that to survive in my family and in the world I would have to get rid of these impulses. So I did. Slowly I shoved them so far back into my consciousness that I forgot they were there at all.

These "bad qualities" became my shadow. And the older I got, the further back I pushed them. By the time I was a teenager, I had shut down so much of myself that I was a walking time bomb waiting to explode on anyone who got in my way. Along with the so-called bad qualities, I had also pushed back all their positive opposites. I could never experience myself as beautiful because I spent so much time trying to hide my ugliness. I could never feel good about my generosity because it was just a mask to cover my greed. I lied about who I was, and I lied to myself about what I was capable of achieving. I lost access to all of who I was.

Because I had worked so hard to shut myself down, I had no patience for others who might be exposing their imperfections. I became intolerant and judgmental. As far as I was concerned, no one was good enough, the world was an awful place, and everyone in it was in trouble. I believed my problems were being imposed on me because I was born into the wrong family, had the wrong friends, the wrong face, the wrong body, lived in the wrong town, and went to the wrong school. In my heart, I truly believed these external circumstances were the cause of my loneliness, anger, and discontent. I thought, "If only I had been born into wealth like I deserved, lived in Europe, and went to boarding school. If only I had the right clothes and a big bank account, my world would be fine. All my troubles would vanish."

I had fallen into the all-too-familiar trap of "if only." If only this was like that, everything would be okay. I would be okay. This delusion didn't last long. When the fantasy dried up I was faced with my worst nightmare. I found out that all I was . . . was me: skinny, imperfect, middle-class, angry, and selfish. It has taken me seventeen years to come to terms with all of who I am. The brilliant and the beautiful, the imperfect and the flawed. And it still takes work, even to this day.

The reason for doing shadow work is to become whole. To end our suffering. To stop hiding ourselves from ourselves. Once we do this, we can stop hiding from the rest of the world. Our society nurtures the illusion that all the rewards go to the people who are perfect. But many of us are finding out that trying to be perfect is costly. The consequences of emulating the "perfect person" can eat away at us, physically, mentally, emotionally, and spiritually. I've worked with so many good people who suffer from various dis-eases . . . addiction, depression, insomnia, and dysfunctional relationships. They are people who never get angry, never put themselves first, never even pray for themselves. Some of their bodies are riddled with cancer and they don't know why. Buried in their bodies, stuffed far back in their minds, are all their dreams, anger, sadness, and desires. They were raised to put themselves last because that is what good people do. The hardest thing for them is to break free from this conditioning, to find out who they really are. Because they are deserving of their own love, they are deserving of forgiveness and compassion, and therefore deserving enough to express their anger and their selfishness.

Within ourselves, we possess every trait and its polar opposite, every human emotion and impulse. We have to uncover, own, and embrace all of who we are, the good and bad, dark and light, strong and weak, and honest and dishonest. If you believe you are weak, then you must seek out its opposite, and find your strength. If you are ruled by fear you must go within and find your courage. If you are a victim you must find the victimizer inside you. It is your birthright to be whole: to have it all. It only takes a shift in your perception, an opening of your heart. When you can say "I am that" to the deepest, darkest aspect of yourself, then you can reach true enlightenment. It's not until we fully embrace the dark that we can embrace the light. I've heard it said that shadow work is the path of the heart warrior. It takes us to a new place in our consciousness where we have to open our hearts to all of ourselves, and to all of humanity.

In a recent seminar, a woman stood up crying. Her name was Audrey. She was in tremendous pain. She had terrible thoughts, she admitted, and was ashamed and embarrassed to share them because then we would know she was a truly bad person. After a long discussion, she finally confessed that she hated her daughter. She was so upset I could hardly hear what she was saying. She repeated it softly, over and over: "I hate my daughter." Everyone in the room was looking at her, some with compassion, others in horror.

I worked with Audrey for a while, explaining that if hate was what she was feeling, it was okay. She needed to accept the hate she felt for her daughter. I asked how many other people in the room had children. Almost everyone raised a hand. I asked them to close their eyes and try to remember a time when they might have felt hate for their children. Everyone found at least one memory of feeling hate. Then I had them imagine what gift hate could give them. Some said sanity, some said love, and others said release of emotion. Everyone saw that they had no control over the emotion itself. Even when they didn't want to feel hate, they felt it sometimes.

Seeing that she was not alone helped Audrey give herself permission to feel hate without judgment. I explained that we all needed hate to know love, and that hate only has power when it is suppressed or denied. I asked Audrey what would happen if she embraced her hateful feelings and waited to find their gifts instead of suppressing them. She still looked ashamed, her head down, so I told her a story.

One day, twin boys went off with their grandfather on an outing. They walked through the woods until they came upon an old barn. When the boys and their grandfather stepped inside to explore, one of the boys immediately started complaining: "Grampa, let's get out of here. This old barn stinks like horse manure." The boy stood near the door, angry because he now had manure on his new shoes. Before the old man could respond he saw his other grandson running happily through the barn's many stalls. "What are you looking for?" he asked the second little boy. "Why are you so happy?" The boy looked up and said, "With all that horse manure in here there must be a pony somewhere."

The room was now quiet. Audrey's face was shining. She was beginning to see the gift of her hatred—the pony—in this aspect of herself. This shift in perception allowed the negative energy she had carried around for years to be released. Audrey understood that her hateful feelings were a defense mechanism, which protected her boundaries around the people she loved. Even though this hate had caused her great pain, it had also been the catalyst for her spiritual journey and the impetus for her to seek out her own inner truth.

There was more gold to come. Two weeks after the course Audrey's daughter called her. Audrey was feeling good about herself so she took a risk and told her daughter how she had felt for the past couple of years. Audrey explained how she had embraced her hateful feelings in the course, and when Audrey finished speaking, her daughter started crying. She cried and cried, releasing years of pain and emptiness, and expressed all the hate she had felt for her mother. When she was done she asked her mother to meet her for lunch. Sitting across from each other, they were able to feel the special connection that a mother and daughter have, and they vowed to express any and all emotions from then on so that nothing would ever keep them apart again.

If Audrey hadn't been brave enough to express her hate, this healing wouldn't have been possible. Both mother and daughter had so many suppressed emotions that anytime they got into a room together, there would be a blowup. The hate needed to be expressed and embraced so that its gift could be revealed. The gift of Audrey's hate was love. It gave Audrey a new, beautiful, honest relationship with her daughter.

Every aspect of ourselves has a gift. Every emotion and every trait we possess helps show us the way to enlightenment, to oneness. We all have a shadow that is part of our total reality. Our shadow is here to point out where we are incomplete. It is here to teach us love, compassion, and forgiveness, not just for others but also for ourselves. And when the shadow is embraced, it can heal us. It is not just our denied "darkness" that finds its way into the recesses of our shadow. There is a "light shadow," a place where we have buried our power, our competence, and our authenticity. The dark parts of our psyches are only dark when they are stuffed away and hidden. When we bring them into the light of our consciousness and find their sacred gifts, they transform us. Then we are free.

I saw this clearly in one of my courses in a tough, resistant, gum-chewing woman with "screw you" invisibly tattooed across her forehead. Pam questioned everything, yet firmly stated she had no problem owning her darkness. She was right: her darkness was her comfort zone. She did not care if you called her angry or a bitch. Pam considered those words compliments. So when I told Pam she was a "mush-pie," she looked at me in disgust and complete disbelief. "Me? Mushy? Never!" She was completely unable to see herself as soft, sweet, or feminine. I left her alone, trusting the weekend process would show her the way. Sure enough the next day, after a cathartic movement meditation, I asked several people to come to the middle of the group to get a hug from the rest of us. I had never done this before, but it was clear that Pam and a few others were stuck and needed some love. When we put our arms around her Pam broke down, wailing inconsolably and calling for her mother. For more than an hour a group of ten or so people sat comforting Pam while she let go of years of pain, loneliness, and sadness.

Although it seemed like her tears would never end, Pam finally surrendered and allowed us to love her unconditionally. Later, I discovered Pam had been abandoned during infancy and had never met her mother, nor did she have a single baby picture of herself. In fact, she had hired a private investigator who had been trying to locate her mom for the past several years. By the last day of the course Pam was embracing her softness and gentle qualities. Everyone kept marveling at her transformation. And just a week later, Pam heard from the private investigator and received her first baby picture. Two weeks after that, the detective found her mother, and Pam spoke with her for the first time. Once the shadow is embraced, it can be healed. When it is healed it becomes love.

If the gold is in the dark, then most of us have been looking in the wrong place. As Deepak Chopra often says, "Within every human being there are gods and goddesses in embryo with only one desire. They want to be born." We long to see the seeds of our divinity blossom but we have forgotten that every seed needs fertile ground in which to grow. That dark, earthy, essential place within us is our shadow. It is a field that needs acceptance, love, and cultivation before the flowers of ourselves can bloom.

EXERCISES

It's important to be in a state of mindfulness when you do these exercises. All the answers you need are within but you must become quiet enough to hear them. Leave yourself plenty of time, and make sure you turn off your phone and completely surrender to the process. I recommend that you set aside at least one hour to do these exercises. Put on comfortable clothes and sit in your favorite place in your house. You might want to light some candles and put on soft music to help create a seductive atmosphere for yourself. Nearby, keep a journal and a pen or pencil that you enjoy writing with. You might want to get a tape recorder and record the following steps so you won't have to keep opening your eyes to read what comes next.

When you're ready, close your eyes and take five slow, deep

breaths. Inhale for five counts, retain the breath for five counts, and then exhale slowly through your mouth. Use your breath to relax your entire body. Focus all your attention on your breath as you continue. This is one of the best ways to quiet your mind.

Now, with your eyes shut, imagine yourself walking into an elevator and closing the door. Press one of the buttons in the elevator and go down seven floors. Imagine you're going down deep into your consciousness. When the door opens you see a beautiful sacred garden. Try to clearly visualize everything about it. Notice the trees, the flowers, the birds. What color is the sky? Is it a brilliant, clear blue or is it laced with clouds? Feel the air's temperature and the wind caressing your cheeks. How are you dressed? Are you wearing something you love? Imagine yourself at your best, looking your most attractive. Take off your shoes and feel the earth beneath your feet. Is it grassy or sandy? Is it dry or moist? Do you see a pathway of stone or marble? Are there waterfalls or statues? Are there any animals? Take a minute to look around in all directions and notice what else is in your garden.

When you've finished creating your garden, create a sacred meditation seat where you can come to find all the answers you've ever desired. Spend a minute exploring your inner sacred place and make a commitment to visit it often. Return your attention to your breath and take five more slow, deep breaths. Bring yourself to an even deeper state of relaxed awareness.

Now ask yourself the following series of questions, and take your time in listening to your inner voice. After each question open your eyes for a moment and write down your answers in your journal. The best way to do this is to write fast and to write whatever comes to your mind. There are no right or wrong answers. Don't worry about what you are writing; just let yourself feel and express whatever needs to emerge through this process. When you have the answer to the first question, close your eyes, return to your garden, and sit down in your meditation seat. Take two more slow, deep breaths before you ask yourself the second question and so on. Take your time.

1. What am I most afraid of?
2. What aspects of my life need transforming?
3. What do I want to accomplish by reading this book?
4. What am I most afraid of that someone else will find out about me?
5. What am I most afraid of in finding out about myself?
6. What's the biggest lie I've ever told myself?
7. What's the biggest lie I've ever told someone else?
8. What could stop me from doing the work necessary to transform my life?

When you finish this exercise allow yourself time to write in your journal and express on paper anything else that needs to surface. Then take a moment to acknowledge the courage and hard work you brought to this exercise and continue on to the next chapter.

CHAPTER 3

THE WORLD IS WITHIN US

W e are not in the world, the world is within us." The first time I heard this, I was puzzled. How can the world be within me? How could it be possible that you, another human being, could live inside me? It took a long time to understand that what is actually inside me are the thousands of qualities and traits that make up every human being and that beneath the surface of every human is this blueprint of all mankind. The holographic model of the universe teaches us that each of us is a microcosm of the macrocosm. Each of us contains all the knowledge of the entire universe. If you cut the hologram on your credit card or driver's license into tiny pieces and shine a laser beam on one of them, you will see the entire picture. In the same way, if you examine one human being you will find a hologram of the universe. This universal blueprint resides in our DNA.

Dr. David Simon, medical director of the Chopra Center for Well Being and author of *The Wisdom of Healing,* explains it this way: "A hologram is a three-dimensional image derived from two-dimensional film. The unique feature of the hologram is that the entire three-dimensional picture can be created out of any piece of the film. The whole is contained in every bit; that is why it is called a hologram. In a similar way, every aspect of the universe is contained within each of us. The forces that comprise matter throughout the cosmos are found in each atom of the body. Every strand of my DNA carries the entire evolutionary history of life. My mind contains the potential of every thought that ever was or will be expressed. Understanding this reality is the key to the door of life—the entrance way to unbounded freedom. Experiencing this reality is the basis of real wisdom."

When you understand that you contain everything you see in others, your entire world will alter. Our goal in this book is to find and embrace everything that we love and everything that we hate in other people. When we reclaim these disowned aspects of ourselves, we open the door to the universe within. When we make peace with ourselves we spontaneously make peace with the world.

Once we accept the fact that each of us embodies all the traits in the universe, we can stop pretending that we are *not* everything. Most of us were taught that we are different from other people. Some of us consider ourselves better than others, and many of us believe that we are inadequate. Our lives are molded by these judgments. It is these judgments that lead us to say, *"I am not like you."* If you grow up white you might believe you are different from African Americans. If you grow up African-American you might believe you are different from Asians or Hispanics. Jews believe they are different from Catholics, while right-wing conservatives believe they are different from left-wing liberals. Each of our cultures has taught us to believe that we are fundamentally different from the rest. We also adopt prejudices from our families and friends. "You're different because you are fat and I am skinny. I am smart and you are stupid. I am timid and you are brave. I am passive and you are aggressive. I am loud and you are soft spoken." These beliefs maintain the illusion that we are separate. They create internal as well as external barriers that keep us from embracing the totality of our being. They keep us pointing our fingers at others.

The key is to understand that there is nothing we can see or perceive that we are not. If we did not possess a certain quality we could not recognize it in another. If you are inspired by someone's courage, it is a reflection of the courage within you. If you think someone's selfish, you can be sure that you're capable of demonstrating the same amount of selfishness. Although these qualities will not be expressed all the time, we each have the ability to act out any quality we see. Being part of the holographic world we are all that we see, all that we judge, all that we admire. Regardless of skin color, weight, or religious preference we share the same universal qualities. All humans are the same in this essential way.

Renowned Ayurvedic doctor Vasant Lad says, "Within every drop is the ocean and within every cell is the intelligence of the whole body." When we grasp the enormity of this we can start to see the vastness of who we are. Men and women are created equal in that they share the same full range of human qualities. We all have power, strength, creativity, and compassion. We all have greed, lust, anger, and weakness. There is no trait, quality, or aspect that we don't possess. We are filled with divine light, love, and brilliance, and equally filled with selfishness, secrecy, and hostility. We are meant to hold the entire world within us; part of the task of being fully human is to find love and compassion for every aspect of ourselves. As is the human mind, so is the cosmic mind. Most of us are living with a narrow vision of what it is to be human. When we allow our humanity to embrace our universality, we can easily become whatever it is we desire.

In *Love and Awakening*, John Welwood uses the analogy of a castle to illustrate the world within us. Imagine being a magnificent castle with long hallways and thousands of rooms. Every room in the castle is perfect and possesses a special gift. Each room represents a different aspect of yourself and is an integral part of the entire perfect castle. As a child, you explored every inch of your castle without shame or judgment. Fearlessly you searched every room for its jewels and its mystery. Lovingly you embraced every room whether it was a closet, a bedroom, bathroom, or a cellar. Each and every room was unique. Your castle was full of light, love, and wonder. Then one day, someone came to your castle and told you that one of your rooms was imperfect, that surely it didn't belong in your castle. They suggested that if you wanted to have a perfect castle you should close and lock the door to this room. Since you wanted love and acceptance, you quickly closed off that room. As time went by, more and more people came to your castle. They all gave you their opinions of the rooms, which ones they liked and which ones they didn't. And slowly you shut one door after another. Your marvelous rooms were being closed off, taken out of the light, and put into the dark. A cycle had begun.

From that time on, you closed more and more doors for all kinds of reasons. You closed doors because you were afraid, or you thought the rooms were too bold. You closed doors to rooms that were too conservative. You closed doors because other castles you saw did not have a room like yours. You closed doors because your religious leaders told you to stay away from certain rooms. You closed any door that did not fit into society's standards or your own ideal.

The days were gone when your castle seemed endless and your future seemed exciting and bright. You no longer cared for every room with the same love and admiration. Rooms you were once proud of, you now willed to disappear. You tried to figure out ways to get rid of these rooms, but they were part of the structure of your castle. Now that you had shut the door to whatever room you didn't like, time went by until one day you just forgot that room altogether. At first, you didn't realize what you were doing. It just became a habit. With everyone giving you different messages about what a magnificent castle should look like, it became much easier to listen to them than to trust your inner voice: the one that loved your entire castle. Shutting off those rooms actually started to make you feel safe. Soon you found yourself living in just a few small rooms. You had learned how to shut off life and became comfortable doing it. Many of us also locked away so many rooms that we forgot we were ever a castle. We began to believe we were just a small, two-bedroom house in need of repairs.

Now, imagine your castle as the place where you house all of who you are, the good and bad, and that every aspect that exists on the planet exists within you. One of your rooms is love, one is courage, one is elegance, and another is grace. There are endless numbers of rooms. Creativity, femininity, honesty, integrity, health, assertiveness, sexiness, power, timidity, hatred, greed, frigidity, laziness, arrogance, sickness, and evil are rooms in your castle. Each room is an essential part of the structure and each room has an opposite somewhere in your castle. Fortunately, we are never satisfied being less than what we are capable of being. Our discontent with ourselves motivates us in our search for all the lost rooms of our castle. We can only find the key to our uniqueness by opening all the rooms in our castle.

The castle is a metaphor to help you grasp the enormity of who you are. We each possess this sacred place inside ourselves. It is easily accessed if we are ready and willing to see the totality of who we are. Most of us are scared of what we will find behind the doors to these rooms. So instead of setting out on an adventure to find our hidden selves, full of excitement and wonder, we keep pretending the rooms don't exist. The cycle continues. But if you truly desire to change the direction of your life you must go into your castle and slowly open each and every door. You must explore your internal universe and take back all that you've disowned. Only in the presence of your entire self can you appreciate your magnificence and enjoy the totality and uniqueness of your life.

When I began my search for the world within me I thought it was an impossible task. I thought the world was a mess but that I was not. I thought, *I am not a murderer. I am not a homeless person.* I didn't really want to find out that I possessed *all* the qualities of the world. As far as I could see I was nothing like the people I judged or made wrong. My goal became that of seeing how the world could exist within me. Every time I saw something or someone I didn't like, I started saying to myself, "I am like that, they are within me." For the first month I was disappointed because I truly couldn't find any of the "bad" things in myself.

Then one day while I was riding on the train everything changed. A woman in my car was yelling at her child. I was busy telling myself I would never treat my child that way and how awful this woman was for scolding her child in public. When a little voice in my head said, "If your child had just spilled chocolate milk all over your white silk suit you would throw a flying fit." Suddenly the pieces of the puzzle fell together. Of course I had the ability to get angry at a child. I didn't want to admit that to myself, so when I saw someone else fly into a rage, I was judgmental instead of empathetic. This took the focus off me. I realized that it was the *quality* demonstrated by each person that was within me, not the person herself. I am not the angry woman on the train, but I do possess the impatience and intolerance that she revealed at that moment.

What I discovered was my potential to act like the people I had been most harshly judging. It became clear that I had to be on the lookout for the traits that most bothered me in others. I began to recognize them as rooms I'd closed off. I had to acknowledge that I, too, could yell at my child if I had a bad day. Then I looked at a homeless person and asked myself, "If I had no family or no education and I lost my job, would it be possible for me to be homeless?" The answer was yes. If I changed the circumstances of my life, it was easy to see I could do and be almost anything different.

I tried being every kind of person: happy, sad, angry, greedy, and jealous. Fat people had been a special target of mine. My father had always been heavy, and he was included in my prejudice. Suddenly he looked different to me. I was born with thin bones and a fast metabolism. I realized that if my metabolism changed and I continued to eat the junk I ate, I would be fat too. But there were still a few areas where I was having difficulty. I could never imagine myself being a murderer or a rapist. How could I kill someone in cold blood? It was easy to imagine killing someone if he tried to hurt me or my family but how about those brutal, senseless crimes? I realized I had no desire to kill now, but if I had been locked in a closet for fourteen years and beaten every day would I be able to kill in cold blood? The answer was yes. This did not make killing acceptable, but it allowed me to see that I could truly embrace the possibility of being everyone.

When I had trouble being anything from that day on I would break it down. For instance, I still could not see how I could ever be a pedophile, so I asked myself what *kind* of person would have sex with a child? A degenerate, fearful, perverted person, I thought. Then I asked myself, "Could I be a degenerate? Could I be fearful? Could I be perverted?" I tried to imagine the worst circumstances that could have happened to me as a child and I realized that if I was abused and violated as a child and had lived without love I would have grown up differently. Under those circumstances there was no way I could predict what I would and would not be capable of doing. Don't judge a man until you have walked in his shoes. Even though some of these characteristics were hard for me to own, I had to face the possibility that a demon lived inside me. Sometimes the question is not whether you have a specific trait at the moment but whether you could display that trait under different circumstances.

I tried on every kind of person that disgusted or repulsed me. Some were harder to accept than others, some took more time, but eventually there was little I could not own within myself. Over time my inner voice that went through life judging everything and everyone had quieted. Silence of the mind is something I had dreamed about my whole life and now I was seeing the possibility emerge. I realized that I only judged people when they displayed a quality I could not accept in myself. If someone was a show-off, I no longer judged them because I knew that I, too, was a show-off. Only when I had completely convinced myself that I was not capable of a certain behavior would I get upset and point my finger at the other person. Hold your hand straight out in front of you and point at someone. Notice that you have one finger pointing at them and three fingers pointing back at yourself. This can serve as a reminder that when we are blaming others we are only denying an aspect of ourselves.

The process of hiding and denying parts of myself began to seem almost comical once I realized all the energy I was using in order to *not be* a certain kind of person. If you don't see yourself as a microcosm of the entire universe you'll continue to live your life as a separate individual. You'll look outward instead of inward for answers and direction, and make judgments about what is good and what is bad. You'll maintain the illusion that you and I are not really connected. You'll stay behind your mask in order to feel safe and secure. But if you embrace the totality of the universe within yourself, you embrace the totality of the human race.

Recently, I went to Colorado to lead a seminar for a couple, Mike and Marilyn, and their marketing company. When I arrived at their house, we went out for a quick lunch with their children to discuss emotional-release work. At lunch we had a wonderful discussion about living in a world where we all recognize that each of us has an imprint of the entire universe within. Mike and Marilyn were already familiar with the holographic theory and were enthusiastic. But when we got into the car after lunch, Mike turned around and said to me, "But there are a few things I know I'm not." I wasn't surprised; this often happens after someone agrees that they are everything. It had happened to me after all. So I asked Mike, "What aren't you?" Mike replied, "I'm not an idiot." I looked into the rearview mirror where Mike was looking straight at me and said, "If you're everything, then you're also an idiot." There was dead silence in the car. Mike's wife and children were all looking at me in disbelief. I had told Mike he was an idiot. Then Mike started to tell me about all the idiots he knew and how he wasn't like any of them. He was so emotional about the people he was describing that I knew this was a very charged issue for him.

We continued driving while Mike exhausted his repertoire of idiot stories. Finally I asked him, "Have you ever done anything that an idiot might do?" He thought about my question and quickly said yes, but again he went on to tell me how I couldn't compare what he'd done with what the idiots he knew had done. These other people were really big idiots. I told him that the psyche couldn't distinguish between a small idiot and a big idiot—an idiot is an idiot. Because the word "idiot" was so charged for him, I asked Mike if he thought that this might be a signal telling him something. Needless to say, it was a very long ride.

I asked Mike at least to consider my point that idiocy was an aspect of him that he had rejected at some point, and now had an opportunity to reclaim. How could he be everything but an idiot? And what was wrong with being an idiot, anyway? I asked his wife and children if any of them cared if I called them an idiot. No one else had any charge on the word. I asked if any one of them were having bad experiences with idiots. No one was.

When we arrived at their house we bundled up to get out of the car. It was eighteen below zero outside. I had never been in weather this cold, so I stood there stunned, shivering, waiting for the front door to open. A few minutes went by while Mike fumbled around in his pockets and then groped in the car. Finally, Mike looked at us and said, "I think I locked the keys inside the house." After a moment's silence, I asked, "What kind of person would lock himself out of his house in eighteen-degree-below-zero weather?" We all simultaneously screamed, "An idiot!" Mike laughed, and Marilyn eventually found her key and got us into the house. Once again, the universe assisted me in my work.

After we warmed up, I sat down with Mike to see if he could identify when he had made the decision not to be an idiot. He remembered doing something stupid as a child and being laughed at. At that time he vowed to himself never again. He shut down a room in his castle because he thought it was bad. As Gunther Bernard so aptly said, "We choose to forget who we are and then forget we've forgotten."

Aspects that are hidden from ourselves, like idiocy from Mike, have a particularly powerful influence on our present reality. They have a life of their own and are always trying to get our attention in order to be accepted and integrated into our whole self. Mike kept unconsciously attracting idiots into his life so that he could experience this disowned aspect of himself. Mike could not find compassion for his own mistakes, so he saw people who made mistakes as idiots. Hating this aspect of himself, he hated anyone else with the same flaw. This influenced how he managed people at work. His employees perceived him as difficult and sometimes irrational.

I suggested to Mike that this disowned aspect of himself that he called "idiot" came bearing gifts. I had him close his eyes and tell me the first word that came to mind when I asked, what is the gift of being an idiot? He replied, determination. Because Mike didn't want to be considered an idiot, he had worked very hard at school and became a great student. He went to college and then on to get his master's degree, and became an accountant. He worked hard to be at the top of his field and kept up on local and world news events as an educated person would. Mike was a little shocked by what he was saying. I asked him if "idiot" had given him all of his determination to get where he had gotten in life, would he be willing to forgive and embrace this aspect of himself? With some hesitation he said he would, although he'd need some time to digest our conversation.

The next day Mike seemed younger and more vibrant. He still wasn't sure that owning and loving this aspect that he called idiot was the right thing to do since he had spent nearly forty years denying it to himself. But after another long conversation he could see that because he didn't own this aspect of himself he attracted many people into his life who did act like idiots. I explained that this is a spiritual law—that the universe always guides us back to embracing the totality of ourselves. We attract whomever and whatever we need to mirror back the aspects of ourselves that we've forgotten.

Each aspect within us needs understanding and compassion. If we are unwilling to give it to ourselves how can we expect the world to give it to us? As we are, so is the universe. Self-love must sink in and nourish each level of our being. There are those who love their inner selves but are unable to look into a mirror for more than a minute at their outer appearance. Other people spend all their time and money on their outer selves and end up hating what's inside. The time has come to bring the whole of yourself into the light so that you can choose to consciously shift every area of your life, internal and external. Now is the time to be the idol of yourself. Every part of you has something to give you. By loving and embracing all of yourself, you will truly be able to love and embrace all of us.

EXERCISES

Start by clearing away anything that might distract you. You'll need your journal, crayons, and a pen. You might want to put on some soft music to help you relax. Now close your eyes and take a slow, deep breath. Use your breath to quiet your mind and surrender to the process. Take five more slow, deep breaths.

Meeting Your Sacred Self

Imagine again an elevator within you. Step into the elevator and go down seven floors. When you step out of your elevator you will see your beautiful garden. Walk through your garden and notice the flowers and trees surrounding you. Look at the lush green leaves and savor the rich smells of the flowers. It is a beautiful day and the birds are singing. Notice the color of the sky. Remember how comfortable and safe you feel in your garden. Take a moment and take another deep breath, inhaling the beauty of your sacred garden. Find a quiet place to sit and create a comfortable meditation seat. A place where you feel your best. Make sure you put on clothes that caress your body and make you feel desirable and magnificent. Then sit down and close your eyes. In a moment, an aspect of yourself will come into your consciousness. This aspect will be you at your best. It will be the totality of who you are, filled with love and compassion and with power and strength. This aspect of you is your sacred self. Invite this magnificent being to fully enter into your awareness. Visualize yourself manifesting your highest potential, feeling peaceful and silent, centered and fulfilled.

Now ask your sacred self to sit down next to you. Take this aspect by the hand and look it in the eye. Ask it if it will be there for you to guide you and protect you this week. Then ask it what you need to do to open your heart and let go of any old emotional toxicity you have been carrying around. Now embrace this sacred aspect of yourself and thank him or her for coming to see you, and vow to revisit him or her and your garden often.

Now open your eyes and write about your experience in your journal. What you saw, what your garden looked like, how you looked and felt. What did your sacred self look like? What did he or she have to say? Take your time. The longer you write, the more wisdom will be expressed through you. Then take out a piece of paper and some crayons and draw a picture of your sacred self. Don't worry about what your picture looks like; this is not a coloring contest. Just give yourself permission for at least five minutes to draw.

Meeting Your Shadow

Close your eyes and take five very slow, deep breaths. Inhale to the count of five, retaining your breath for as long as you comfortably can and then exhale as slowly as possible. Use your breath to quiet your mind and go deep within your consciousness. Imagine yourself going into an elevator and down seven floors. When you open the door to the elevator you see a very dark and dingy place. Imagine the worst possible circumstances. Notice the smells, the filth, the garbage everywhere. You might be in a cave filled with rats, snakes, cockroaches, or spiders. Call forth a place that you wish never to go to. When you've created this place, continue to take slow, deep breaths and then look down into a corner and see the lowest form of yourself imaginable. Allow an image of you at your worst to appear in your mind. Try to sense and see everything about you: how you look, how you smell, how you feel. Now allow a word that describes the person you are seeing to come into your mind. After you have visited with this person long enough to get a sense of him or her, open your eyes. Write down the word you received and everything you experienced in your visualization. Write for at least ten minutes. Allow your consciousness to express whatever thoughts or feelings it has about your experience.

Sacred Self Embracing Shadow Self

Close your eyes and return to your sacred garden. Create a safe, sacred environment to do your exercises in. Again, use your breath to quiet your mind and to bring you deeper into your consciousness. Now take your internal elevator down seven floors and go into your garden. Walk through and admire its beauty. When you feel the soothing presence of your surroundings, find your meditation seat. When you are comfortable and feel safe, bring forth the image of your sacred self. Imagine basking in all of his or her light. When that image is established, go in and call forth the dark, shadowy aspect of yourself. Ask your sacred self to come and embrace your shadow self. Allow this all-loving, beautiful part of you to hold this scary, dark, unloved part in his or her arms. Imagine sending love, kindness, and forgiveness to your dark side. Tell this dark aspect of yourself that it is safe and that you are going to spend time understanding and learning to love it. Spend as much time as you need and don't be upset if your shadow self does not allow itself to be embraced. Go in and try daily until it does. Often our resistance will show up in visualization, so after ten minutes or so, say good-bye to both of these aspects and come back into your room.

Take out a piece of paper and some crayons and draw a picture of your experience. You should spend about five minutes on it. When you've finished, take out your journal and write about your meditation and your drawing experience for at least ten minutes.

CHAPTER 4

RE-COLLECTING
OURSELVES

Projection is a fascinating phenomenon they failed to teach most of us about in school. It is an involuntary transfer of our own unconscious behavior onto others, so it appears to us that these qualities actually exist in the other people. When we have anxiety about our emotions or unacceptable parts of our personalities, we attribute these qualities—as a defense mechanism—to external objects and other people. When we have little tolerance for others, for example, we are likely to attribute the sense of our own inferiority to them. Of course, there's always a "hook" that invites our projection. Some *imperfect* quality in other people activates some aspect of ourselves that wants our attention. So whatever we don't own about ourselves we project onto other people.

We see only that which we are. I like to think of it in terms of energy. Imagine having a hundred different electrical outlets on your chest. Each outlet represents a different quality. The qualities we acknowledge and embrace have cover plates over them. They are safe: no electricity runs through them. But the qualities that are not okay with us, which we have not yet owned, do have a charge. So when others come along who act out one of these qualities they plug right into us. For example, if we deny or are uncomfortable with our anger, we will attract angry people into our lives. We will suppress our own angry feelings and judge people whom we see as angry. Since we lie to ourselves about our own internal feelings, the only way we can find them is to see them in others. Other people mirror back our hidden emotions and feelings, which allows us to recognize and reclaim them.

We instinctively draw back from our own negative projections. It's easier to examine what we are attracted to than what repels us. If I am offended by your arrogance it is because I'm not embracing my own arrogance. This is either arrogance that I am now demonstrating in my life and not seeing, or arrogance that I deny I am capable of demonstrating in the future. If I am offended by arrogance I need to look closely at all areas of my life and ask myself these questions: When have I been arrogant in the past? Am I being arrogant now? Could I be arrogant in the future? It would certainly be arrogant of me to answer no to these questions without really looking at myself, or without asking others if they have ever experienced my being arrogant. The act of judging someone else is arrogant, so obviously all of us have the capacity to be arrogant. If I embrace my own arrogance, I won't be upset by someone else's. I might notice it, but it won't affect me. My arrogance outlet will have a cover plate on it. It is only when you're lying to yourself or hating some aspect of yourself that you'll get an emotional charge from someone else's behavior.

When I began to lead seminars I was petrified. Every week, I would stand in front of a group and try desperately to be myself. Fearful that I would not be liked I worked hard at being authentic. The seminars I was leading at the time were in Oakland, California, where two out of three participants were African-American. I was excited to be going into a new community, and I was committed to supporting participants in their goals. When I began leading my third seminar, one of the participants stood up, and with an edge in her voice Arlene began to share. As soon as she started speaking, strong feelings emerged from deep within me. It was difficult for me to hear what this woman was saying because I was too busy feeling angry. I thought, if all this woman is going to do is give me a hard time she should sit down and shut up. It was unusual for me to find myself reacting to a participant. I went home upset and tried to embrace in myself the qualities I saw in this woman—nasty, angry, aggressive, and mean.

For the next four weeks, every time I led a session, Arlene would stand up and be condescending and a bit rude. I found myself spending much of my free time trying to figure out why this woman got me so upset. No matter how I tried I couldn't stop judging her. One day, feeling defeated, I called a woman in the seminar whom I worked closely with and asked her why Arlene hated me. Susan replied, "Debbie, don't worry about her; she's just a racist." I hung up the phone, feeling weak and nauseous. I quickly affirmed, "I'm not a racist." I thought about all my childhood memories of African-American friends in my life. I remembered teaching them how to swim and running track with them. I thought of my father and how he'd fought for civil rights: he had the first black law partner in the state of Florida. I felt sure I was not a racist.

That night, as I lay in bed thinking about the next session of my seminar, I kept hearing Susan's words, "She's just a racist." Over and over these words rang in my ears. Just as I was about to fall asleep, I heard a voice in my head asking, "What did you think about Arlene the first time she stood up and gave you a hard time?" Suddenly, I felt pressure in my chest and feared the worst. What I remembered thinking was, *You stupid black bitch.* These words resonated through my body. I thought, *It couldn't be, I'm not a racist. I wouldn't think that thought, I couldn't mean it.* My heart raced with fear. But I sat alone, confronted with my own racist statement. This was my shadow.

I cried with shame for hours, feeling a deep sense that I had betrayed all my friends in Oakland who loved and trusted me. No matter what I did I was unable to acknowledge, "I am a racist." Everything I believed about possessing every trait went out the window. I spent hours in front of a mirror saying, "I am a racist, I am a racist," trying to accept this part of myself, trying to find some comfort.

The more I repeated the words the easier it became. Knowing there was a gift somewhere in those words I began to look for it. Then I remembered my father talking endlessly about equal rights and how none of us would be free until we realized that we were all equal. This passion of my father's had become a passion of my own. I saw that not wanting to be a racist had pushed me to work hard to form relationships with African-Americans. It also gave me a deep need to support people who were discriminated against. At the time all this took place I was actively involved in raising money for an organization called Prison Possibilities, which helped primarily minority inmates transform their lives. When I finally embraced the idea of being a "racist," I felt like I had released sixty pounds from around my neck.

The next night, I went to my seminar feeling whole and hopeful. In the middle of the seminar Arlene raised her hand like she did every week. Feeling hesitant, I called on her to share. We were talking about the next community seminar so I was particularly nervous about what she would say. I wanted everyone to continue to participate. When Arlene stood up she smiled and said, "This is a great seminar," and then she shared her breakthrough experience with all of us. When Arlene sat down I was shocked.

I drove home thinking about the dramatic change in Arlene's behavior. I didn't want to get too excited so I decided to wait and see how things went the following week. Next week came, and as the seminar progressed I waited for Arlene to raise her hand. When she stood up Arlene once again acknowledged that the seminar was making deep changes in her life. Then she acknowledged my being supportive of and committed to the Oakland community. At the end of the evening I stayed to talk to several people. Out of the corner of my eye I could see Arlene standing close by chatting with some friends. I turned to her and looked into her eyes and asked, "What happened?" She looked back at me and said, "I don't know. Last week I walked in the room and I just fell in love with you."

This experience changed my life and proved to me once and for all that when you embrace a quality within yourself, other people with the same quality can no longer plug into you. Then they become free to experience you and you are free to experience them.

Ken Wilber makes a great distinction in the book *Meeting the Shadow*. He says, "Projection on the Ego Level is very easily identified: if a person or thing in the environment *informs us,* we probably aren't projecting; on the other hand, if it *affects us,* chances are that we are a victim of our own projections." If you truly understand this you will never see the world the same way again. Think about it this way. If someone walks by you and spits on the sidewalk and you notice but don't react, it probably isn't something you need to work on. But if you get upset and think, *How could someone be so uncouth and disgusting?*, then you are projecting. You may be engaged in some disgusting behavior now or may have demonstrated some disgusting behavior in the past. For some reason disgusting behavior is not okay with you, so you are *affected* by the behavior of the spitter. All of this might have started when you were small. Perhaps you actually did spit and someone said, "That's disgusting." Maybe someone in your family spit and others reacted to it in a negative manner. Whatever happened, you made a decision never to do anything like that, and pushed this aspect of yourself way back into your consciousness. If this person who spits affects you it should trigger your internal alarm. These alarms are clues to uncovering your dark side. With this in mind, you can look at what emotionally affects you as a catalyst for growth, giving you an opportunity to reclaim a hidden aspect of yourself.

At this point many of you might be saying, "This is ridiculous. I don't want to find out I'm disgusting or arrogant." You have to remember there's a gift in each of these aspects. But in order to receive the gift, you first have to uncover, own, and embrace these aspects. There's an old Sufi story about a philosopher who made an appointment to debate with Nasrudin, a Sufi wisdom teacher. When the philosopher arrived for his appointment he found Nasrudin away from his home. Infuriated, the philosopher picked up a piece of chalk and wrote "Stupid Oaf" on Nasrudin's gate. When Nasrudin got home and saw this he rushed right over to the philosopher's house. "I had forgotten," he said, "that you were to call. And I'm sorry I missed our appointment. But, I remembered our appointment the minute I saw that you had written your name on my gate."

Our indignation over the behavior of others is usually about an unresolved aspect of ourselves. If we listen to everything that comes out of our mouths when we talk to others, judge others, or

give advice, we should just turn it around and give it to ourse...
The philosopher could just as easily have written "rude oaf," "in-
considerate liar," or "backstabbing coward." On the other hand, he
could have come to a totally different conclusion and been afraid
that Nasrudin had been hurt in an accident or had fallen ill. But
the words that came to him when Nasrudin was not home were
"stupid oaf." When we have a trait that doesn't have a cover plate
over it we draw incidents into our lives to help us own and embrace that denied aspect. Without being influenced by a single
fact other than Nasrudin's absence, the philosopher projected his
own unembraced trait of "stupid oaf."

We project our own perceived shortcomings onto others. We
say to others what we should be saying to ourselves. When we
judge others we are judging ourselves. If you constantly beat yourself up with negative thoughts, you will either beat up on the people around you—verbally, emotionally, or physically—or you will
beat up on yourself by destroying some area of your own life.
What you do and what you say is no accident. There are no accidents in the life that you create. In this holographic world, everyone is you and you are always talking to yourself.

When you call someone a name for making a mistake, stop
and think whether you would call yourself the same name. If you
are being honest the answer will invariably be yes. The world is a
giant mirror always reflecting back parts of ourselves. Every trait
is there for a reason, and all traits are perfect in their own ways.

Not long ago I noticed that I was asking everyone I know how
often they meditate, and for how long. Then I would remind them
of the importance of meditating every day and spending at least a
half hour a day going within oneself. Eventually, I asked myself
why I was being so adamant about the meditation practice of
other people. When I examined my motives I realized that I often

skipped my own meditation practice. A part of me was starving to spend more time going within and being silent. Since I had a three-year-old child at home, I had somehow rationalized that it was okay every time I skipped my daily meditation. When I realized I was only telling others what I needed to hear myself I was able to take back my projections and honor my unconscious desire. I started meditating more and stopped pushing others to do what I needed to do myself. This is why I often say, "Attend your own lectures." When I examined my motivation for telling people to meditate, I recognized my own need.

Our shadows are often hidden so well from us that it's nearly impossible to find them. If it weren't for the phenomenon of projection they might stay hidden from us for a lifetime. Some of us buried these traits when we were three or four years old. Think about playing in your home when you were small, and imagine hiding a coin. Twenty, thirty, or forty years later, it would be nearly impossible to remember the incident itself, let alone where you hid the coin. When we project onto other people we have an opportunity to finally find that coin.

When my nieces come to visit me from Dallas, I always pay a lot of attention to what they're eating. When we go out to restaurants I try to steer them towards foods that are low in fat. Then when I think they've eaten too much I discourage them from ordering dessert, which they love. Often I tell them we'll go for low-fat dessert later. During their last visit, we all stood around my kitchen talking about what we project onto other members of our family. We went around the room taking turns and had a lot of fun telling each other which person had the honor of receiving our negative projections. When it was my turn I suddenly realized that this obsession with my nieces' eating habits was my own projection. I was dissatisfied with my own unhealthy eating, so whenever they came to town I pretended there was nothing wrong with me and everything was wrong with them. I'm tall and thin, so I can pretend I eat well even when I don't. But as soon as I realized it was not about them but about me, I could deal with the real issue. This made room for me to have a better relationship with my nieces. Suddenly it didn't matter to me what they ate. We could just go out and enjoy each other's company.

You can't just look at areas of your life that you think aren't working. You want to find all the places where you deceive yourself. One place where I frequently run across hidden issues is with people trying desperately to avoid being like their mother or father in some aspect. If your mother was strict, you might become lenient. If you grew up in a poor home, you might have a powerful drive to be rich. If your parent was domineering, you might be passive or too tolerant of others' behaviors. If your father was unfaithful, you might become very loyal, and if one of your parents was lazy, you might become a workaholic. I could go on and on, but the point is that acting in reaction to your parents is often just a disguise.

One of my clients hated her father because he was so cheap. Holly had spent her entire adult life trying to avoid being cheap by buying fabulous presents for everyone in her family. And she was always inviting friends out for dinner and shows and paying for everything. Holly was proud of the fact that she was so generous. When I told her that she needed to embrace her own impulses to be cheap in order to forgive her father and let go of her resentment, she was unwilling to see herself that way. For weeks we discussed her life, with Holly noting how generous she was being with everyone. Then one day, Holly called me from the supermarket. She realized she had just spent almost an hour looking at different products, comparing prices and the amount of product in each container so that she could save pennies. It astonished her that she would spend $500 on a sweater without thinking twice but that she wasn't willing to pay an extra twenty cents for a box of Kleenex. Suddenly the bell went off for Holly. She realized she was cheap just like her dad, only in a different way. The shock of discovering this aspect of herself left her in tears. So much of Holly's energy was spent on not being like her father. She had hidden her impulses to be cheap for so many years, and suddenly here they were inside her, just as clear as day.

After some time Holly was able to appreciate the gift of being cheap. For Holly, "cheap" turned out to be the part of her that made her want to plan for her future and invest money for her retirement. Until this point Holly had been unable to save money because she was too busy being unlike her father. She was also able to be much more accepting of her father, which brought them closer together than ever before.

Freedom is being able to choose whoever and whatever you want to be at any moment in your life. If you have to act in a particular way to avoid being something you don't like, you're trapped. You've limited your freedom and robbed yourself of your wholeness. If you can't be lazy, you can't be free. If you can't be angry when something upsetting happens, you can't be free. If you deal with someone's behavior by being the opposite, question yourself. If you are constantly annoyed by a particular group of people, find the ways in which you are like them. It's not only our negative traits that we project onto other people; it's also our positive traits. Most people whom I work with project their genius and creativity, their power and success. If you want to be like others, it's because you have the ability within you to be like them. If you are enthralled by megastars and spend time and money reading about their lives, find the aspect you love in them inside of you.

You deserve to have whatever it is you see and truly desire. The only difference between you and the people you idolize is that they are manifesting one of the qualities you desire and probably fulfilling their dreams. When you are not living up to your potential, it's easy to project your positive traits onto people who are living up to theirs. When you start to fulfill your own dreams and goals you'll become less interested in what other people are doing. We each need to become our own hero. The only way to do this is to take back the parts of us that are plugged into someone else, the parts of us that we have given away.

For almost a year I have been working with a friend who brings my Shadow Process to Miami. Rachel is young, beautiful, bright, and talented. Whenever Rachel and I are together she makes a big deal out of me, always acknowledging and complimenting me. She is forever telling me how brilliant, talented, and beautiful I am. Although I know that Rachel does love and respect me, I also know that she is projecting her own brilliance, talent, and beauty onto me.

Keenly aware of the process of projection, I have resisted her infatuation. Instead, I have guided her in reclaiming her disowned brilliance, beauty, and talent. After many discussions, it was clear that Rachel believed I possessed some qualities that she lacked. Assuring her this wasn't true, I asked her to search and name the aspects she attributed to me. We know projection is taking place when someone is emotionally affected by another's behavior, whether positive or negative. In this case, Rachel is affected by my positive traits. Rachel is seeing her own capacity in me. I am her mirror. Since she is not yet living up to her desired potential, she is only able to see her light shadow through me. This leaves Rachel in a difficult position. If I leave her, these parts of her disappear: they go back into the dark until she finds someone else to project them onto. The qualities in me that affect her are only an image of what is possible for herself.

As long as we deny the existence of certain traits in ourselves, we continue to perpetuate the myth that others have something we don't possess. When we admire someone, it is an opportunity to find yet another aspect of ourselves. We have to take back our positive projections as well as our negative projections. We have to remove the plugs we've attached to others, turn them around, and plug them back into ourselves. Until we are able to retrieve our projections it is impossible for us to see our full potential and experience the totality of who we really are.

If I'm attracted to Martin Luther King's courage it's only because I am seeing the amount of courage I am capable of expressing in my life. If I'm attracted to Oprah Winfrey's influence it is because I'm seeing the amount of influence I am capable of having in my life. Most people project their greatness. This is why actors and famous athletes make so much money in this country. We are paying them to be our heroes—to act out our unfulfilled dreams and desires. People envy these stars without knowing anything about their personal lives. They get lost in their idol's life as a way of avoiding their own. The deeper truth is that they are projecting an aspect of themselves onto their hero. If you see greatness, then it is your own greatness you are seeing. Close your eyes and think about this. *If you admire greatness in another human being, it is your own greatness you are seeing.* You may manifest it in a different way, but if you didn't have greatness within, you wouldn't be able to recognize that quality in someone else. If you did not possess that quality you would not be attracted by it. Everyone sees other people differently because everyone is projecting aspects of him or her self. It's our job to distinguish what inspires us about others and then take back those aspects of ourselves we have given away.

People often wonder how they can be like someone they admire when at this moment their lives may look so very different. For example, they might say they admire Michelangelo but they are sure they are not like him. What they really need to do is focus on exactly those qualities that inspire them to want to be like Michelangelo. It might be his artistic talent if they are unexpressed artists. It might be his courage, his creativity, or his genius. Their talent might not be in art but they have the ability to be as great, as creative, and as courageous in their unique expression of their gifts. They might manifest their talents in music, photography, or gardening.

Any desire of the heart is there for you to discover and manifest. Whatever inspires you is an aspect of yourself. Be precise about what you admire in someone and find that part in yourself. If you have the aspiration to be something, it's because you have the potential to manifest what you are seeing. Deepak Chopra says, "Within every desire is the mechanics of its fulfillment." This means we have the ability to manifest our heart's desires and that which we are. If we are not capable of doing or having something we will not have an authentic yearning for it. It's as simple as that. Goethe said, "If we can conceive it, and we can believe it, then we can achieve it." The difficult part is working through our fears. Our fears stop us. They tell us we're not good enough or worthy enough. There is no one on the earth like you. No one with exactly the same desires, the same talents, or the same memories.

You have your own individual spin on everything. It is your job to discover your unique talents and then manifest them in your own unique way.

Several months ago, my friend Nancy who had been in a slump for years came to visit. I invited her to hear one of the top motivational speakers in the world. During the lecture we were both quiet; I was busy taking notes. When we got into the car to go home, Nancy turned to me and said, "That guy is such a loser." Shocked, I asked her why she believed that. She told me she thought he was full of it and that he had no idea what he was talking about. He spoke too fast and looked like a nerd. For the rest of the ride home Nancy pointed out everything she didn't like about this man's manner and message. When we arrived home I asked Nancy to come and sit down with me. I asked her if she really believed this man was a loser. She looked at me with certainty in her eyes and said yes. Taking out a sheet of paper, I asked if she'd be willing to look at this issue. She thought about it for a moment and decided to play along.

On one side of the paper I wrote down all the things I knew about this man. He has a successful business as a consultant for Fortune 500 companies. He sells countless motivational tapes, and is paid over $5,000 a night to speak. He has been married for more than twenty years and has three healthy children. On the other side of the page, I wrote down what I knew about Nancy's life. She was divorced with no children. She had little contact with most of the members of her family. She was unemployed and had been unsuccessful in starting her own business several times. She was overweight and out of shape, and suffered from several ailments. She had debts of more than $50,000, and was currently living hand-to-mouth. Nancy looked at my list. Now I said, "If I brought ten people in and showed them these lists who do you think they would call the loser?"

At first, Nancy drew back, horrified that I or anyone was calling her a loser. This was her worst nightmare. But I explained that until she owned this aspect of herself she'd always project it onto other people. Nancy would be unable to hear important, powerful messages from other people because she was projecting her denied thoughts onto them. After a couple of hours, Nancy began to see that deep within herself she believed she was the loser. This thought was so painful to her that she buried it very deep. Her father had told her she would never amount to anything and she had believed him. Since her childhood she had been unconsciously creating situation after situation in her life to prove she was a loser in order to retrieve this aspect of herself which she had disowned. It was always mirrored back to her in the external world but she would deny it, and the cycle would continue. Once Nancy recognized her belief that she was a loser, then she could begin to look for the gift of this aspect and embrace it. Then Nancy would be able to examine how she'd set herself up to lose, and make a new commitment to honor the loser in herself and allow the winner in herself to create a life of abundance. Nancy has since started a new career, and has been enjoying tremendous personal and financial success.

There is an old saying, "It takes one to know one." We see in others what we like and don't like in ourselves. If we embrace these parts of ourselves we will be able to see others as they are, not as we see them through our cloud of projection. There is another saying that the three greatest mysteries of the world are air to birds, water to fish, and man unto himself. We are able to see everything in front of us in the outside world. All we have to do is

nd look around. We cannot see ourselves. We need
ee ourselves. You are my mirror and I am yours.

EXERCISES

1. For one week, observe your own judgments about other
   people. Whenever you are upset by another person's
   behavior, write down the quality in him or her that is
   most upsetting to you. Write down any opinions you have
   of the people who are closest to you. Be sure to include
   your friends, family, and co-workers.

   This list marks the beginning of discovering your
   hidden aspects. You will refer to it when you start the
   process of owning your shadow.

2. Make a list of the advice you give to other people. What
   are you telling others to do to make their life better?
   Reflect on whether the advice you give to others isn't just
   advice to yourself. Sometimes we tell other people what
   to do as a way of reminding ourselves what we need to
   do. Realize that your advice to them may be a way to
   remind yourself.

CHAPTER 5

KNOW THY SHADOW, KNOW THY SELF

Within each of us lies a solid gold treasure. This golden essence is our spirit, pure and magnificent, open and glowing. But this gold has been covered up by a hard shell of clay. The clay comes from our fear. It is our social mask: the face we show the world. Unconcealing your shadow reveals your mask. We must look at this mask with love and compassion for there is great value in understanding what we hide behind.

Consider the story of the Golden Buddha. In 1957, a monastery in Thailand was being relocated and a group of monks was put in charge of moving a giant clay Buddha. In the midst of the move one of the monks noticed a crack in the Buddha. Concerned about damaging the idol, the monks decided to wait for a day before continuing with their task. When night came, one of the monks came to check on the giant statue. He shined his flashlight over the entire Buddha. When he reached the crack he saw something reflected back at him. The monk, his curiosity aroused, got a hammer and a chisel and began chipping away at the clay

Buddha. As he knocked off piece after piece of clay, the Buddha got brighter and brighter. After hours of work, the monk looked up in amazement to see standing before him a huge solid-gold Buddha.

Many historians believe the Buddha had been covered with clay by Thai monks several hundred years earlier before an attack by the Burmese army. They covered the Buddha to keep it from being stolen. In the attack all the monks were killed, so it wasn't until 1957, when the monks were moving the giant statue, that the great treasure was discovered. Like the Buddha, our outer shell protects us from the world: our real treasure is hidden within. We human beings unconsciously hide our inner gold under a layer of clay. All we need to do to uncover our gold is have the courage to chip away at our outer shell, piece by piece.

In my seminars I often work with people who have invested in years of therapy, transformational seminars, breath work, and other healing modalities. They ask the same questions: "When will it end? When will I be done? How much more work must I do on the issues that come up over and over again?" These people are not looking at themselves as magnificent Buddhas encased in clay shells. These people hate their shells. They haven't discovered that their clay shells protect them in more ways than they can imagine. We need our shells for many reasons, and for each of us the reasons may be different. Even though our ultimate goal is to shed our shells we first need to understand and make peace with these masks. Do you think after the monks chiseled the shell off the gold Buddha, the Buddha angrily said, "I hated that horrible shell"? Or do you think the Buddha blessed the shell that served to protect him from being stolen away from his home?

When I was young my outer shell was tough, uncaring, and insensitive. Saying "I've got it all together" hid my feelings of inadequacy and gave me the illusion that I was okay. As I chiseled away at my shell, piece by piece, my shining essence began to emerge. But it was not until I could distinguish those aspects that made up my shell, as a cover-up for many hidden emotions, that I was able to see past my tough exterior. Once I started looking through the cracks I was able to let go of my shell. And when I came to appreciate and respect this hard shell for protecting me, my life was transformed.

Your outer shell is the you who faces the world. It hides the characteristics that make up your shadow. Our shadows are so well disguised that we often show the world one face when, in fact, the exact opposite is really within us. Some people wear a layer of toughness that hides their sensitivity, or a mask of humor to cover up their sadness. People who know it all are usually covering up feelings of stupidity, while those who act arrogantly have yet to reveal their insecurity. The cool people are hiding the geek within, and the smiling face, an angry one. We have to look beyond our social masks in order to discover our authentic selves. We are masters of disguise, fooling others but also fooling ourselves. It's the lies we tell ourselves that we need to decipher. When we're not completely satisfied, happy, healthy, or fulfilling our dreams, we know these lies are in our way. This is how we recognize our shadow at work.

The shift that needs to occur is perceptual. You need to see your outer shell as having served as protection, not just something that keeps you from fulfilling your dreams. Your outer shell is divinely designed to guide your spiritual process. By revisiting and exploring each incident, emotion, and experience that led you to construct that shell, you'll be guided back home to embrace the totality of your being. Our shells are the road map to our personal growth. They are made up of all that we are, and all that we don't want to be. No matter how painful your past or present might be, if you look at yourself truthfully and use the information stored in your outer shell as a guide, it will lead you in your journey towards enlightenment.

When you get to know your whole self, you will no longer need your shell to protect you. You will naturally allow your masks to fall away, exposing your authentic self to the world. You will not have to pretend that you're more or less than anyone else. Everyone in the world can become your peer. Our shells are created from our ego ideal. The ego is the "Self" distinguished from other. Spirit combines "self" and other as one. When this union between spirit and self occurs, we become one with ourselves and one with the world. Most people don't get very far unconcealing their shadow because they're unwilling to be honest with themselves. The ego doesn't enjoy losing control. The moment you acknowledge all aspects of yourself, the good and the bad, the ego begins to feel a loss of power. In *The Tibetan Book of Living and Dying,* Sogyal Rinpoche explains that

> the ego is our false and ignorantly assumed identity. So ego, then, is the absence of true knowledge of who we really are, together with its result: a doomed clutching on, at all costs, to a cobbled together and makeshift image of ourselves, an inevitably chameleon charlatan self that keeps changing and has to, to keep alive the fiction of its existence.

If you begin the process of unconcealing your shadow and a voice inside starts screaming for you to stop, know that it's only your ego fearing its own death. Give yourself permission to uncover your true self. Challenge the person you think you are in order to unveil the person you are capable of becoming.

Using other people as mirrors helps you to decipher your mask. Go out and interview people close to you—friends, lovers, family, and colleagues. Ask them which three things they like the most about you and which three things they like the least. It's important for the people you're asking to know it's okay for them to be honest. You're the only one who can make it safe for others to tell you the truth. Find out if you appear to others the way you appear to yourself. Other people often see more positive aspects in us than we see in ourselves, and at the same time they see more negative traits than we see, or admit to ourselves.

People often resist this exercise. They fear being judged. The word judgment carries a lot of baggage, so I prefer to use the word feedback. Feedback is a useful tool. We never have to believe what others think about us, but if we are afraid to hear what the people closest to us have to say, we should take notice. Most people are afraid they will hear what they fear most. This is denial at work. Think of denial as an acronym for Don't Even Notice I Am Lying. We only fear feedback if we know on some level that we've been lying to ourselves. If you honestly feel that what someone thinks about you has no basis in reality, you won't care. We care when we've been deceiving ourselves and get called on it. Take Kate, for example.

Kate came to do some work with me and when I asked her to do this exercise, many of the people she interviewed said she lacked integrity. She was baffled because her whole life, as she saw it, had been about being honest at all costs. Knowing how this process works, I was sure the people around her perceived some aspect of Kate that she had hidden from herself. I asked her to close her eyes and allow images to come to her mind whenever I asked her a question. After we consciously took several deep breaths together I put on some music and began to guide her through a visualization. I asked her to go for a walk in a garden. I had her imagine beautiful plants, trees, and flowers there. When Kate was relaxed and comfortable, I asked her to remember a time when she had been dishonest, a time when she had lied or cheated, a time when she had no integrity. We sat in silence. Then tears began rolling down her cheeks. When Kate finally spoke, she recounted this story.

Kate had wanted to be a doctor her entire life. She had finished her last year of medical school and was in her third month of residency at a large hospital in New Orleans. It was dinner time in the hospital and everyone was busy. Kate was in a hurry too. She was making rounds, looking in on her patients. She entered a woman's room and decided she wanted to flush a line around the woman's heart with saline. Kate couldn't find a nurse to help, so she rushed down the hall herself to get a tube of saline solution. Without looking at the tube a nurse had given her, Kate injected the solution into the line. Halfway through the procedure, the woman whom she was injecting the fluid into went into a seizure. Shocked, Kate looked down at the tube in her hand and saw that the label said potassium chloride. She stopped the injection immediately and stabilized the woman until she came out of the seizure. By this time, many of the staff doctors had come to try to figure out what happened to this patient. Kate had already hidden the tube. She was horrified. Because she broke one of the fundamental rules taught in medical school—never give medicine to a patient without first checking the label—she could have killed or seriously injured this woman. When the doctor asked Kate what happened she lied and said she didn't know. Until this moment, Kate had never told anyone this story. In fact, she had never thought about it since the day she finished her residency and left that hospital. On that terrible day, Kate swore that she would never make a medical mistake again.

In the sixteen years since that incident, Kate became a world-famous physician and author, proud of her integrity and full of distaste for anyone with standards lower than her own. But in her personal life, what kept coming up was Kate's friends questioning her integrity. Because she'd disowned this part of herself, buried it long ago, she was blind to it. Kate wore a mask of integrity to hide the part of herself that was deceitful. She had fooled herself into believing her own disguise.

This single act of dishonesty, which Kate had not come to terms with, took on a life of its own. When she lied to others in her relationships she was unable to see it. She complained that she was always being misunderstood. And despite all her accomplishments, Kate was never satisfied with her life. She feared intimate relationships, keeping her friends at arm's length to make sure no one discovered her secret. She thought she loved herself but after our work together she could see there was a part she hated, an aspect of herself that once caused her shame and humiliation. Once Kate was able to see and own her lack of integrity, a light went on inside her. She was now able to see the other places in her life where she'd lied to herself or to others. When we finished our work, Kate looked years younger. She was able to release the giant lie she'd suppressed in herself. She felt light and free, but didn't understand why. This is how I explained her physical sensation of release.

Think for a moment about how much energy it takes to hide something from yourself and the world. Try taking a piece of fruit, say, a grapefruit, and carry it around in your hand the whole day. Keep the grapefruit out of your own sight and make sure when you are around other people that you hide the grapefruit so they cannot see it. After a few hours, notice how much energy you're expending. This is what our bodies have to do all day long. Except they don't have just one piece of fruit, they have to deal with all of the pieces of fruit you're trying to hide from yourself and from the world. When you finally allow these truths about yourself to surface, you'll be free. You'll have all that excess energy to spend on your personal growth and on the path to achieve your highest goals. We are only as sick as our secrets. These secrets make it impossible for us to be our authentic selves. But when you make peace with yourself, the world will mirror back that same level of peace. When you're in harmony with yourself, you'll be in harmony with everyone else.

Other people listen to what you're saying, and see what you're doing, but they are also conscious of your body language and whether or not it contradicts what you say and do. So it's important to look closely at what you're physically communicating to others. As Emerson said, "Who you are speaks so loud, I can't hear what you're saying." What are you saying when you're not speaking? Our body language, our facial expressions, and the energy we give off are constantly sending out messages. Recent studies show that 86 percent of our communications are nonverbal. That means that only 14 percent of what you say verbally makes any difference to those you are speaking to. You want to ask yourself: "What am I communicating in the silence? What are the messages I am sending out? Do I have a smile on my face when I feel sad? Do I look mad when I am telling you how great my life is? Do I believe I'm in great shape when my mirror tells me something else? Can I look into my eyes and feel good about what I am seeing or do I run away?"

These are often difficult questions to confront. You have to give yourself the freedom to not like your answers, because inevitably there will be unpleasant ones. But they'll be the most useful. Recently, I worked with a group of people who were being trained to lead seminars on healing. We were videotaping everyone so they could see how they appeared to other people. An attractive young woman named Sandra got up to speak. While her words were beautiful, all I could take in was the way she swayed—her slow, sensual movements that flirted with the audience. When she finished her talk, I asked her how she thought people perceived her. She replied, as competent and loving. When we asked the rest of the group, they made comments like "cute," "sexy," "has a lot of attention on herself." I told her that if I were a man, I'd want to have a drink with her after the seminar. As a woman, I might be offended by her sexy movements. Everything she was doing was distracting us from what she was trying to communicate. Sandra's goal was to provide people with information so that they could heal themselves. But all we could hear her saying was, "Look at how beautiful and sexy I am. Do you like me? Do you find me attractive?" All this was unspoken, but nonetheless, the audience was thinking about Sandra's body instead of the message she wanted us to hear. We played back Sandra's video without any sound and she was shocked by what she was communicating. When I asked her why she thought she was doing this she said she wanted people to like her, and she got her power by attracting men to her. The truth was that her body language was actually depleting her power. Sandra had been studying for years to be a healer. Now she finally had the opportunity to speak in front of large groups, and she was presenting them with her mask rather than her message. Sandra was more than willing to see and hear the truth even though she felt angry and embarrassed by her performance. She worked hard on owning her silent communications and the part of herself that needed so much approval from men. As soon as she uncovered this aspect of herself, Sandra was able to embrace it and subsequently became a great speaker who could fulfill her dream of helping people.

Interviewing others to find out how they perceive you is a scary process. But every bit of feedback is a blessing. It takes courage and commitment to see all of yourself. If you're unwilling to hear the truth, you'll be unable to transform your life. People often go through a kind of grieving process after they've discovered parts of themselves that had been hidden for a long time. If you've been fooling yourself about your level of self-love, you've got to let yourself feel sad or angry for a while. Remember the core of your being: the whole of who you are doesn't change as you transfer certain emotions and impulses to your shadow. You never actually become a different person; the true, wonderful you always exists way down, deep inside. So coming to terms with your shadow is a way of remembering who you really are.

Now that we've received feedback from others let us continue the process of unconcealing our shadow. Another way to expose your hidden aspects is to make a list of three people you admire and of three people you hate. The people you admire should inspire you with qualities you'd like to emulate. The people you don't like should get you really angry or upset. They would have done something which you find horrifying. The lists do not have to include people you know, although they can. They can also be politicians, actors, writers, philanthropists, musicians, or killers. After you've made your list, write down the three qualities you like or admire most about each person, and those you dislike or hate the most. Then, on a separate sheet of paper, make a list of all the positive qualities of the people you admire on one side and all the negative qualities you dislike on the other. My list looked like this:

Martin Luther King, Jr.—*visionary, courageous, honorable*
Jacqueline Onassis—*elegant, successful, leader*
Arielle Ford (my sister)—*spiritual, creative, powerful*

Charles Manson—*predator, fearful, hateful*
Hitler—*murderer, prejudice, evil*
Harriet Spiegel (an old teacher)—*arrogant, know-it-all, angry*

POSITIVE LIST	NEGATIVE LIST
visionary	predator
courageous	hateful
honorable	fearful
elegant	murderer
successful	evil
leader	prejudice
spiritual	arrogant
creative	know-it-all
powerful	angry

These lists are a good place to find disowned aspects of yourself. Carefully go over each trait you've listed. I like to start with the negative traits first. In the beginning you might have trouble seeing how you have the same traits as someone like Hitler. It is important to break down any general word, like murderer. The question to ask is, What kind of person would commit these acts? For example, for murderer, you might say selfish, enraged, doesn't value human life. If you come up with a phrase like "doesn't value human life," then ask yourself what kind of person has no value for human life. You might come up with sick, demented, and narcissistic. The important part of this process is to break the language down until you get to a specific word or a quality that you hate or dislike. Find the qualities that give you an emotional charge. Determine what plugs you in.

Steven, a successful business consultant who came to one of my seminars, had been meditating for eight years, and made a real commitment to alter his life. He hadn't had a relationship for the past five years and was ready to find a partner, get married, and start a family. He felt ready to dig inside himself and to try to find out why he'd been so unsuccessful in love. By the second day, Steven had unconcealed many aspects of himself but there was one thing bothering him. On a break, he called me over to tell me there was a gentleman in the seminar he could not stand. I asked him what he disliked so much about this other man. He only thought about it for a second, then whispered in my ear, "He's a wimp, and I hate wimps." I didn't say a word but stood there quietly until Steven was ready to speak. There was a glimmer of recognition in his eyes as he told me this story. When Steven was five years old his father had wanted him to go on a pony ride. They were at a state fair with his entire family. Steven had never seen a real pony and was awfully scared of this big animal. When Steven told his father he didn't want to go on the pony ride because he was scared, his father had scolded him: "What kind of man are you going to make? You're nothing but a little wimp, you're an embarrassment to our family." Steven was punished. Since that day, Steven made a decision never to be a wimp again. He spent the rest of his life trying to make his father proud. He became a black belt in karate, played college football, lifted weights, all to prove he wasn't a wimp. He'd managed to fool his father, but he'd also learned to fool himself. He'd forgotten this painful incident.

I asked Steven if he could see any area in his life where he was still a wimp. After some thought he said he was a wimp about women. He was afraid of women, of communicating honestly with them, so whenever there was a problem in a relationship Steven just left. He'd left almost every women he'd ever been in a relationship with, and at this point he was even scared to ask attractive women out. I told Steven to take some time to fully feel his shame and his embarrassment.

When I asked Steven what the good thing was about being a wimp, he looked at me like I was crazy. He couldn't comprehend how something this horrifying, something he'd spent his whole life denying, could be a gift. But then Steven remembered a time when being a wimp had probably saved his life. When he was in college, a group of his friends had gotten together to do some drinking. They'd been going at it for a couple of hours when one of the guys suggested going to a bar in the next town. Steven's three other friends decided they should all go. Steven was scared to drive drunk or to be in a car with anyone who was drinking and driving, so he told his buddies he had a date and was going to get laid. He didn't want to tell them he was scared to go. He didn't want to be a wimp. Two hours later, his friends drove off the road, one of Steven's closest friends was killed, and the other three were seriously injured.

Steven couldn't believe what he was remembering. He had blocked this painful incident from his mind. At the time of the accident he figured it was just luck that he had skipped out that night. I asked him if there were other times when being a wimp had kept him out of trouble. He could see now how this trait had made him a cautious man, had kept him out of fights, and had probably saved him from all kinds of trouble. We talked about many past incidents before I asked Steven how he felt about being a wimp now. His face lit up. He had embraced it. He could see now that this aspect of himself had been valuable many times. Steven could now be proud of it. The shame and the pain disappeared.

Steven's new perspective empowered him. We do not have any say about the events of our lives, Nietzsche commented, but we do have say over how we interpret them. Interpretation can really ease our emotional pain. Inventing interpretations is a creative act. As soon as Steven could love and respect his wimpiness he was able to stop projecting it onto other men. Instead of being repelled by wimpy behavior he could be informed by it.

Later in the course, Steven got to know the man that he thought was a wimp. He was amazed at how different this man seemed to him. Had Steven changed that much or had this man changed in only a couple of hours? When Steven owned being a wimp, it changed the lenses he looked through. Now he could see clearly. Letting go of his need to be macho, Steven could accept his sensitivity, shyness, and cautiousness. It let him open his heart and allowed people to get close to him.

Unconcealing is the first step of the shadow process. Unconcealing requires rigorous honesty and willingness to see what you hadn't been able to see. Acknowledgment of our shadow self begins the process of integration and healing. Remember that each of these "negative" traits has a positive gift for you, more value than you can ever imagine. It's only a matter of doing the work, and in a short while you'll receive the blessings of wholeness, happiness, and freedom.

EXERCISES

1. Here's a list of negative words. Take a few minutes and identify any words that have an emotional charge for you. Say out loud, "I am_____." If you can say it without any emotional charge, then move on to the next word. Write down the words that you dislike or react to. If you are not sure that the word has any charge for you, close your eyes for a minute and meditate on the word. Repeat it to yourself a few times out loud and ask yourself how you'd really feel if someone you respected called you this word. If you'd be angry or upset, write it down. Also spend some time thinking about words that are not on this list that run your life or cause you pain.

   Greedy, liar, phony, cheap, hateful, jealous, vindictive, controlling, nasty, possessive, bitchy, wimp, evil, geek, prudish, womanizer, angry, secretive, codependent, alcoholic, predator, drug addict, gambler, sick, fat, disgusting, stupid, idiot, fearful, unconscious, masochistic, bulimic, anorexic, unimportant, shyster, compulsive, frigid, rigid, abuser, manipulator, victim, victimizer, egocentric, better than, foolish, emotional, pompous, ugly, sloppy, loud mouth, big mouth, passive aggressive, smelly, lame, coward, jerk, inauthentic, offensive, inappropriate, wild, dead, zombie, late, irresponsible, incompetent, lazy, opportunist, lush, stingy, unfair, dumb, traitor, weasel, immature, gossip, snippy, desperate, childish, floozy, shrew, pansy, golddigger, hormonal, cruel, insensitive, scary, dangerous, explosive, perverted, psychotic, needy, energy sucker, shit disturber, mean, defensive, man-hater, sad, frail, impotent, insipid, castrated, mama's boy, nervous, arrogant, miser, spinster, slut, deceitful, judgmental, imposter, superficial, violent, thoughtless, martyr, hypocrite, love buyer, sneak, grudge carrier, condescending, competitive, power hungry, wasteful, insane, sinister, bigot, white trash, anxious, stuck, hot shot, goofy, woman-hater, sadistic, nose picker, loser, worthless, failure, envious, critical, flabby, neglectful, whore, shameful, dirty, bitter, shameless, bossy, inflexible, old, cold, withdrawn, soulless, heartless, has-been, cagey, resentful, racist, unenlightened, snob, elitist, faggot, dominating, sleazy, overbearing, inflexible, bad, ignorant, thief, cheater, scammer, pushy, classless, trashy, devious, conniving, groupie, insecure, depressed, hopeless, not good enough, beggar, whiney, asshole, ballbuster, frugal, unlovable, delinquent, scared, hyper, nosy, intrusive, perfectionist, anal, know-it-all, ass-kisser, malicious, resentful, righteous, freak, useless, middle class, resistant, withholding, betrayer, inferior, destructive, thick-headed, confrontational, weak, impatient, full of shit, dyke, self-destructive, imperious, idiot, ruthless, oversensitive, pigheaded, tightass, tasteless, uninteresting, lifeless, empty, diabolical, ridiculous, wretched, pain in the ass

2. Imagine that an article was written about you in your local newspaper. What are the five things you would not want to be said about you? Write them down. Now try to

imagine five things they could say about you that wouldn't matter to you at all. The question is, are the first five things true and the second five untrue? Or, have you decided with the help of your family and friends that the first five things are the wrong things to be, therefore you do not want them said about you? We must uncover what's behind these words, so we can take back these disowned parts of ourselves.

Write down the judgments you have about each of these words. See if you can identify when you first made that judgment or whom you took the judgment from. Was it your mother, father, or another family member?

CHAPTER 6

"I AM THAT"

Once we have unconcealed all of our disowned aspects we are ready to move into the second stage of the process, which is to own all of these traits. By own, I mean acknowledge that a quality belongs to you. Now we can begin to take responsibility for all of who we are, the parts we like and the parts we dislike. At this point, you don't have to like all of your aspects; you just have to be willing to acknowledge them to yourself and others. There are three helpful questions you can ask yourself. Have I ever demonstrated that behavior in the past? Am I demonstrating that behavior now? Under different circumstances am I capable of demonstrating that behavior? Once you answer yes to any of these questions, you have started the process of owning a trait.

Some traits are easier to acknowledge than others. Aspects of ourselves that we've tried hardest to deny or have projected on someone else are the hardest to own. They take more time. But it's just as important to be ruthless with yourself as it is to be gentle.

Be *willing* to find out that you "are" what you least want to be. Be determined to look with new eyes past the defense mechanisms which only want to say, "I am not that." Look through eyes that say, "I am that. Where am I that?" Resist the temptation to judge yourself. Don't jump to conclusions and decide you're an awful person if you find out that you're selfish or jealous. We all possess these qualities as well as their polar opposites. They are a part of our humanity. All of our emotions and impulses—the ones we call positive and the ones we call negative—are there to guide us and teach us. You may be skeptical, but give yourself the opportunity to get to know all these aspects and find their gifts. I promise that you will find gold at the end of this process.

"Owning" is an essential step in the process of healing and of creating a life you love. We can't embrace that which we don't own. If you want to manifest your full potential you have to reclaim the parts of yourself that you've denied, hidden, or given away to others. When I was in the beginning stages of my own healing process I could never find the right man. No one I wanted seemed to want me. I went through men like most people go through magazines. I was attracted to men who weren't right for me because I didn't know who I was, and because I was cut off from so many beautiful aspects of myself. The one man whom I really loved actually told me that he couldn't stay with me because he knew one day I would realize who I was and leave him. My friends could see that the men I picked were wrong for me. But I still believed I was a small two-bedroom house that needed work. So everything and everyone around me kept mirroring back to me my own lack of self-love. Once I owned more aspects of myself—my fear, my covertness, and my grandiosity—I no longer had to attract partners who were fearful, covert, and grandiose. It became easier for me to attract men who could mirror back the positive aspects of myself, men who were kind, giving, and who loved and accepted me as I am.

If there is an aspect of ourselves that we don't accept, we'll continually attract people in our lives who act out that aspect. The universe will keep trying to show us who we really are and to help make us whole again. Most of us have buried these disowned aspects so deep we can't see where we could possibly be a particular kind of person that we look at with distaste. However, if a particular type of person keeps showing up in your life, it's for a reason. For years every time my friend Joanna went on a date she would tell me, "He's not for me, he's a *geek*." The first six or seven times it happened, I didn't say a word. But after a while, it became too obvious. I finally suggested to Joanna that *she* was the geek. I told her that if she owned the geek in herself, she wouldn't find herself dating geeks anymore. She thought I was crazy. I pointed out that I never went out with geeks. How was it possible that all the men she met had this quality which she disliked so much?

So the geek stories went on for months. It became almost comical, because the dynamic was so clear to me and so hidden from Joanna. Then very late one night I got a call from Joanna who had finally had it, after a date with yet another geek. She was really in pain, and asked me to explain to her how she was a geek. I gently suggested that sometimes, when she wore those little pink socks with her white leather sneakers, people might consider her geeky. She half laughed and made me promise that if she owned the geek in herself she would no longer have to date them. She agreed to make a list of all the times in her life she had been a geek. The next day Joanna called me with a long list of geeky things she'd said and done. Because she didn't want to be a geek, Joanna had constructed a "cool" facade. She had been living that way for more than twenty years, but when she looked closely she was able to see that geekiness did rear its ugly head once in a while.

By discovering those geeky moments in her life, and being able to laugh about them with me, Joanna could see that being a bit of a geek wasn't so bad. And since she owned her geekiness two years ago, I can honestly tell you she hasn't been out with a single geek. When she looked to see what her geekiness had given her, Joanna saw that out of her desire not to be a geek she had manufactured a public persona who was cool, chic, and elegant. It was Joanna's geekiness, and her response to it, that had enabled Joanna to create a beautiful style all her own.

There are lots of ways to tackle owning your traits. Start by concentrating on qualities that offend you. Take out your list of words that describe the people you dislike or hate, and examine each trait. No matter how resistant you are, you must own each of these traits in order for the process to work. Find a place in your life where you've displayed this trait or where someone else might have perceived you as embodying this trait. Try on each trait like you would a jacket, see how it feels, and figure out what you have to do to make it fit. Imagine how you would react if you were called that word by someone you love. You have to examine what judgments you make about each trait itself, and what judgments you make about people who possess each trait. Look at how many people you've dismissed for having this aspect. Don't try to compare yourself favorably to these people or to differentiate your behavior from theirs. Don't let your ego try to justify your own behavior. Remember, the world sees a geek as a geek.

A man who attended one of my courses loved the concept of being all things—of having the world within him. Bill was in his late fifties and really only had problems with one person in his life, his twenty-two-year-old son. When I asked what it was that upset him most about his son, Bill said his son was a liar whose constant lying to him was, in his estimation, the worst thing anyone could do. "I've never told a lie my entire life," Bill said. "Ask anyone who knows me." He was so charged up that his face was bright red. For a good fifteen minutes I was unable to help him acknowledge that he'd ever lied in the past, or was capable of lying in the future. Everyone in the course was growing impatient with Bill. The rest of us were able to recall at least a hundred times that we had lied as children, teenagers, or adults, not to mention how often we'd lied to ourselves. But Bill was still not budging. Then I asked Bill if he'd ever cheated a little on his tax returns. A huge smile crossed his face, and with his finger pointing directly at me, he said, "That's a different kind of lying." Everyone in the class looked at him with disbelief.

I'm sorry to say that Bill is one of the few people who took my course but never worked his way through it. James Baldwin, a Jungian analyst, said, "One can only face in others what one can face in oneself." Bill had made his son so wrong for lying and was so self-righteous in his opinion of liars that he was unwilling to discover this aspect in himself. He had too much invested in being right. If Bill had been able to own the aspect of himself that was a liar he would have been able to unplug himself from his son. It takes compassion to own a part of yourself that you've previously disowned, ignored, hated, denied, or judged in others. It takes compassion to accept being human and having every aspect of humanity within you, good and bad. Ultimately, when you open your heart to yourself, you will find you have compassion for everything and everybody.

Last year, a man named Hank came to one of my courses. His big issue was with his girlfriend, who was always late. He shared lots of incidents with the group that had upset him. I suggested that the reason Hank was so upset was that his girlfriend was mirroring an aspect of himself. He told us there was absolutely no way this was possible, though it was quite obvious to everyone in the class that Hank couldn't live with this aspect of his girlfriend. His face was full of disgust when he related how she had stood him up earlier that day, so his feelings were close to the surface. It was the beginning of the seminar, and I didn't want to rush Hank, so I simply told him, "What you can't be with won't let you be." Hank could see he was having trouble accepting his girlfriend's lateness and that he was emotionally plugged in. But when I asked him if he was the kind of person who was ever late Hank's answer was, "absolutely not."

We moved on, going through various exercises, but twenty-four hours later I could see that Hank was still struggling. As the group came back from the second night's dinner break we noticed that one chair was empty. I had asked everyone to come back from breaks promptly so we wouldn't waste any valuable time. We were trying to figure out who was missing when someone said, "It's Hank." We waited a few minutes but Hank was nowhere in sight so we decided to get started. Just then a woman in the front row looked at me and said, "I don't know if you've noticed, but Hank has been late coming back from every break. I, for one, am sick of waiting for him." Suddenly we all realized that Hank was doing to us what his girlfriend did to him. He was making us wait.

When Hank arrived ten minutes later I stopped what we were doing to see if Hank was ready to have a breakthrough. I asked him if he realized he'd been late coming back from every break. He looked at me and said, "I'm only a few minutes late. What's the problem?" Everyone in the room gasped in disbelief. I replied,

"Hank, you are the only person in the room who has been consistently late from five breaks. Some people feel offended that we have to waste time and energy checking to see who's late and then waiting a few minutes to see if you're coming back before we can get started. Can you see any correlation between what you're doing to us and what your girlfriend does to you?" Hank refused to see that his being a few minutes late, meaning anywhere from three to fifteen minutes, was a problem. He told us his girlfriend was often two hours late, or even an entire day late. "That," he said, "is late. That is a problem."

Hank had rationalized a fundamental difference between being five minutes late and being several hours late. For him they were two distinct issues. I asked for a show of hands to see how many people agreed. No one raised a hand. Then I asked how many people felt Hank was being rude by not coming back on time. Everyone raised his or her hand. It was clear to everyone in the room except Hank that he was doing to us what his girlfriend did to him. Late is late, a geek is a geek. It's the ego that makes the distinction to protect itself. Someone stood up and told Hank that they did everything in their power to be on time and they expected other people to do the same. I added that if someone in my life is constantly late and doesn't try to break themselves of the habit I stop making plans with them. I also told Hank that when someone is consistently late I feel like the underlying message they are giving me is my time is not valuable, or that their time is more important than mine. Hank looked upset and perplexed. I asked him to go home that night and think about what we were saying.

The next morning Hank came in on time. He said that he'd stayed up half the night making a list of all the times he'd been late in the past year. He realized that he was almost always late, but he had believed that as long as he was not more than a half hour behind schedule he was doing great. That day, in front of all of us, Hank owned that he was late and that being late was rude. He was still angry at his girlfriend but he could see that in his own way he was doing to us what was being done to him. Hank had buried this aspect of himself so deeply that it was completely hidden from his awareness. Rudeness did not fit into his ego ideal. But as soon as he owned his lateness and rudeness, Hank's face relaxed. He had a natural internal surrender. He could now be with more aspects of himself. And when he spoke about his girlfriend's behavior, it was no longer with total frustration. Hank could see the benefits of taking back his projections from her and owning his own traits. He was becoming free to choose whether he wanted to be in a relationship with a woman who was constantly late.

Hank believed he was a caring and responsible person, but he had needed to attract a particular kind of woman to show him the hidden aspects of himself. People mirror back what is within us because subconsciously we are calling it forth from them. That's why certain kinds of people and situations keep showing up in our lives over and over again. The miracle occurs when you truly own and embrace an aspect of yourself. At that point, the person who is serving as your mirror will either stop acting out the behavior, or you will become able to choose not to have this person in your life. When you unplug, you no longer need another person to mirror your shadow back to you. Because you'll be more whole yourself, you'll naturally gravitate to those who reflect your wholeness. If our soul's purpose is to become complete, we'll continually call forth what we need to see to be whole. As we own more of ourselves, healthier people will show up in our lives.

Take your time in considering what you don't want to own. When resistance to owning something shows up, don't skip over it. Search around until you can see where the resistance comes from. Notice what judgments you make. Write down the times when you've displayed this trait. If you have trouble, enlist a friend to help you. Remember that if you zero in on an unlikable aspect of someone else, it's because you have this same aspect. In my seminars when someone gets stuck on a particular trait and can't seem to own it, I have them own being a "resistant ass." This usually makes people laugh. And when they can be with the resistant ass in themselves, they usually can move quickly through the word that gives them resistance.

The hardest words to own are always related to incidents where we feel someone has wronged us. Our egos resist owning characteristics that would make us give up blaming someone else for the condition of our life. Most of us have spent a long time building cases against the people who have harmed us. Oprah Winfrey once said in a commencement speech, "Turn your wounds into wisdom." Instead of holding onto resentments, learn from them. Look to see how you've benefited from your wounds. Where have they led you? Who is in your life now that might not have been if you hadn't had a particular bad experience? And how does holding onto your wounds keep you from fulfilling your dreams? When you use your wounds to grow and learn, you don't have to continue to be the victim. Look at the person who has harmed you; examine what aspects of this person plug you in. And when you can find those things within yourself, you will no longer be attached to or affected by the other person.

There is a Zen story about two monks journeying home who come to the banks of a fast flowing river. When they reach the riverside they see a young woman unable to cross. One of the monks picks her up in his arms, carries her through the current, and sets her safely on the other side. Then the two monks continue on their travels. Finally the monk who crossed the river alone can restrain himself no longer and he begins to rebuke his brother, "You know it is against our rules to touch a woman. You have broken our holy vows." The other monk answers, "Brother, I left that young woman on the banks of the river. Are you still carrying her?"

When you hold on to old wounds you continue down the road carrying that burden. Recently I worked with a beautiful young woman named Morgan, who had stomach cancer. When she came to see me she had little desire to live and was resigned that her cancer would take her life. Morgan was filled with anger. She hated her mother for the continual cycle of emotional and physical abuse that characterized their relationship. Even though she was in her early thirties and had tried many self-improvement seminars, Morgan had been unable to release the hostility and distaste she had for her mother. So Morgan and I decided that even though she was quite weak, she would give my seminar a try and work on releasing her toxic emotions.

At a certain point in my seminars I ask everyone to write down the five words that are hardest for them to own. We then do a mirroring exercise with partners until each person no longer has any emotional charge on any of their five qualities. For example, if one of my charged words was "incompetent," I would say, "I am incompetent," and my partner, looking me in the eyes, would say, "You are incompetent." Then I would repeat, "I am incompetent," and she would repeat, "You are incompetent." This continues until it no longer matters to me if I am incompetent or if you call me incompetent. Just saying the word out loud, over and over, breaks down our resistance to being called that word and to having that quality.

Before we start, I usually walk around the room and check

people's lists because they often leave off words that are obvious to everyone else, but hidden from themselves. When I arrived at Morgan's seat she was busy owning her words, but I noticed that one word Morgan always used when she spoke about her mother was nowhere on her list. Knowing this was an important thing for her to own, I told Morgan's partner to work on the word "insane."

Morgan looked at me with disgust. She said, "I'm not insane, and you know it." Once again I said if we are everything then how could she not be insane. I told her she could call me insane and I wouldn't mind a bit. Morgan's partner didn't care if we called her insane either. Morgan squirmed, then cried, then told us she felt she might vomit. She couldn't say she was insane. The word could not come out of her mouth. Morgan's partner and I both looked at her and shouted, "Insane! Say it! Own it, Morgan! Insane!" I asked, "Tell me Morgan, when in your life have you been insane?" Morgan recounted a few incidents that clearly could have been considered insane, but the word still stopped her. All I wanted to hear her say was, "I'm insane." I knew if she could repeat this word long enough, it would lose all its energy and the grip it had on her life. What we fear, appears. And for Morgan insanity came in the form of her disease. She had no freedom. But now she was on the brink of owning her greatest fear and nightmare. Morgan went home that night able to say, "I'm insane," but still she did not completely feel it. Later though, after a warm bath and a few hours of saying the word over and over to herself, she got it. A few months later she wrote me a letter:

I had to break any fear and everything that I went through as a child that I associated with insanity to own insane. I had to embrace it and let it go. Once I owned it I dropped to my knees and started praying. Dear God, please remove the scales from my eyes, let me see only the beauty in my mother. For the next 45 minutes I prayed with the most authentic fervor to remove the judgment I had against my mother and myself, to accept that she had done the best she could. I prayed that I could forgive myself for the unconscious blaming, for being hurtful toward myself, for not loving myself and for becoming ill. I was bathed by an exquisite peace. Prior to the work the mere thought of my mother would make me cringe and tense up, now I felt only peace. The exercise had opened the gate, I had walked through it. The cancer stopped spreading and began to slowly recede.

Morgan is now cancer-free. Tests show no signs of the disease. When she stopped hating aspects of herself, she was able to forgive herself and her mother. Today, she tells me that owning the word insane was the hardest part of the process. Her eyes were sealed shut when it came to seeing her mother within herself. But once she realized she was dying of resentment, she allowed herself to embrace the totality of her being. Owning your shadow restores your body's natural tendency toward wholeness. When you are whole you are healed.

Transformation itself only takes seconds. It is a shift in perception, a change in the lenses we look through. If we see the world as if we're a hammer then everything looks like a nail. If we shift from being a hammer to a bolt, then everything looks like a nut. Our perceptions are always colored by how we see ourselves, and the decisions we make about what is good and bad, right and wrong, what we like and what we don't like. If you shift lenses from "I'm in the world" to "I am the world," you will understand that it's not only okay to be everything, but it's essential.

I know this is a difficult concept for most people to accept. We're taught never to say negative things about ourselves. If I wake up feeling worthless, I'm supposed to pretend that I don't feel that way. I'm supposed to say to myself that I'm worthy and hope I will come to feel worthy later in the day. I have to go to work pretending I feel worthy because feeling worthless is not okay. I have to hide behind my mask of worthiness all day, hoping no one will see through it. But, inside, I'll feel a quiet despair knowing I'm not being myself, all because I'm unable to embrace being worthless. We resist this aspect of ourselves and pass judgments on the kind of person that is worthless. We are told affirmations will make us okay. But as I tell people in my lectures if we put ice cream on top of poop after a few spoonfuls we will taste the poop again. When we integrate negative traits into our selves, we no longer need affirmations because we'll know that we're both worthless and worthy, ugly and beautiful, lazy and conscientious. When we believe we can only be one or the other, we continue our internal struggle to only be the right things. When we believe that we are only weak, nasty, and selfish—traits that we believe our friends and families don't possess—we feel shame. But when you own all of the traits in the universe, you'll understand that every aspect within you has something to teach you. These teachers will give you access to all the wisdom in the world.

Sometimes, in order to own a trait, you've got to release some stored-up anger—at yourself, or at others. People often ask me if it's okay to be angry at themselves. My answer is that it's okay to feel whatever you are feeling. Allow yourself to feel and express everything that is within you. You need to get all this negative emotion out before you'll be able to truly love yourself, to feel compassion for yourself and others. You deserve to express your emotions in a healthy way. The only time it's not okay to express your emotions is when you're hurting another person.

Screaming is a good way to let out pent-up emotions. Often our voices have been literally suppressed and we're unable to use our entire vocal range. When you allow yourself to scream completely, with every ounce of your being, you can really clear out repressed energies. If you don't want to disturb anyone, scream into a pillow. If you have never really screamed, or if you grew up in a home where there was a lot of screaming, you may have decided screaming was wrong. Now we're back to "what you can't be with won't let you be." So scream. It's important to have access to your entire range of emotions.

One of my seminars included a beautiful woman in her late sixties who hadn't ever raised her voice in her entire life. Janet had never screamed, never uttered a curse. Her father had drilled into her the idea that nice people didn't do such things and if she was to be respected and loved by him she would have to obey his rules. For sixty years Janet had done exactly what she had been told. And now she was having recurring polyps in her throat. When she finally found me she was ready to release all the emotion that was stuffed inside her and disobey her father. She had come to believe that the cause of her health issues was suppressed emotion. Still, she could hardly raise her voice.

For five days we yelled, screamed, and cursed. Then the moment came when we said the F word. What a release! Janet's whole body shook. The entire next day she walked around with a huge grin on her face. It had taken every ounce of courage she had to do this work even though her father was long dead. Six months later Janet was feeling great and her throat was completely clear. She was expressing herself joyfully and felt she had finally made peace with herself and her father. As long as we are not hurting others we should joyfully express our rage. When you come face to face with an aspect of yourself that you hate, express it. Express it with the intention of releasing all your judgments, your shame, your pain, and your resistance to taking back this disowned aspect of yourself.

My favorite way to release anger is batting. I take a plastic bat and a couple of pillows. Then I kneel down in front of my stack of pillows, raise the bat over my head, and hit those pillows as hard as I can. I imagine that my stack is whatever trait I've resisted owning and whack away. After I release all that emotion, it becomes much easier to go to the mirror and own a trait.

If we embrace it internally we no longer have to create it externally. One of my close friends, Jennifer, was convinced she was being stalked. Jennifer would see this same woman at all the public events she attended. She was sure the woman was following her. "She's evil!" Jennifer would tell me. Of course, being the good friend I am, I told Jennifer, "You are evil." She'd get furious with me and hang up the phone screaming, "I'm not evil!" For nearly a year, this woman kept showing up everywhere Jennifer went and always ruined Jennifer's night. Toward the end of that year, Jennifer flew to Hawaii for a conference. She'd been looking forward to the meeting for months. Sure enough, the woman showed up at the first lecture. Jennifer was horrified. She called me from Hawaii, "What do I have to do to get rid of this woman?" I told her this woman must be mirroring a disowned aspect of herself. It was obvious Jennifer needed to own whatever it was because she was so plugged into this woman. I asked her, "What judgments do you have about being evil?" Jennifer told me of course it was awful to be evil, and evil people did bad things. We tried to think of times in her life she'd been evil, and she came up with a few incidents when she'd done mean things to her little sister that could be considered evil. She had felt deeply shameful of those moments and had decided to be a good person. In her mind good people were not evil. I explained that we couldn't know good without knowing evil, just as we couldn't know love without knowing hate. If we can own the evil or the hate in ourselves, we wouldn't need to project it onto other people.

I told Jennifer to try standing in front of the bathroom mirror and saying to herself, "I am evil," until she no longer cared about denying this aspect of herself. After an hour in front of the mirror, Jennifer was so angry she sat down and wrote a letter to the woman she believed was stalking her. Jennifer allowed herself to call this woman all the nasty names she could think of, to express all her rage. She was radically honest, and as a result she felt lighter and better. Jennifer had needed to give voice to her pain and anger. After writing the letter she tore it to shreds, went back to the mirror, and owned her evil. Once she could face this aspect of herself, she could also face this other woman. She unplugged. When Jennifer saw the woman the next day, she said hello and walked away without being affected at all. She never saw the woman again. This is freedom.

The pain of our perceived flaws compels us to cover them up. When we deny certain aspects of ourselves, we overcompensate by becoming their opposite. Then we create entire personas to prove to ourselves and others that we are not that. Recently, while visiting a close friend I started talking to her father about my work. Norman is a perfect example of this phenomenon. Intrigued, he had asked me to show him what I did. So I asked him to tell me two words he wouldn't want said about him in the newspaper. He replied that he would not want to be called dull or stupid. I laughed out loud. "Exactly," I said. "No one who knows you today would ever say you were dull or stupid." Because he'd always put his family first, Norman had never taken the time to finish his education. But after the death of his wife of more than thirty years, Norman had gone back to school to get a master's degree. He had enrolled in a program at a university near his home and had ridden his bike to school daily. He graduated with honors and is now working toward his Ph.D. When he is not in school, Norman is traveling all over the country, going to conferences and lecturing on physical health and the aging process. He recently went to a Buddhist retreat for a month to get in touch with his spirituality. Would anyone meeting Norman consider him dull or stupid? Everyone I know would call him courageous, interesting, and bright. But Norman's decision not to be dull and stupid actually runs his life, and results in his always competing with himself, to prove that he's not dull or stupid. No matter how hard he works he always has to do more to make sure he's never exposed, and show the world that he's smart and interesting.

It was fairly easy for Norman to recognize how his life is run by the words dull and stupid. He always feels that whatever he achieves is not enough. The irony, of course, is that "dull" and "stupid" have given him his enormous drive and determination. They force him to seek out interesting people and places. If he didn't have this terrible aversion to these two words, we don't know if Norman would have had the drive to do everything he's accomplished in the past four years. Norman perceived the gifts of these two aspects and understood that he is everything. How can we know smart unless we know stupid? How can we know interesting without knowing dull?

When you are internally driven by not wanting to be something, you often become the opposite. This robs you of your right to choose what you really want to do with your life. Norman has no freedom just to take time off and vacation with friends. He won't read a novel or spend an evening playing bridge for fear that he might turn into an old man who is dull and stupid. He cannot look to see if these opportunities are best for his health or for his soul. When you don't own an aspect of yourself it runs your life.

If we look closely, all of us can see where we're dull and stupid. If we're honest, and aren't displaying these aspects right now, then we have to identify a time when we've been dull or stupid in the past. Our opinions of ourselves are the most important opinions. If we feel good about our own lives we seldom care what others say. In Norman's case he has spent the last three years buried in books, working feverishly to be in the top of his class. Some people would say he's dull because all he does is study. Others might say he is stupid to be wasting his time going to school. Until Norman can love the part of him that is dull and stupid and integrate these aspects into his psyche, he will be driven to prove to the world that he is smart and interesting. We exhaust our internal resources when we try *not* to be something.

We are here to learn from all these parts of ourselves and make peace with them. To be truly authentic persons, we have to allow the aspects of ourselves that we love and accept to coexist with all the aspects of ourselves that we judge and make wrong. When we can lovingly hold all of these traits together in one hand, without judgment, they will naturally integrate into our system. Then we can take off our masks and trust that the universe created each of us with a divine design. Then we can stand tall, embracing the world within.

EXERCISES

In order to be completely free, we need to be able to own and embrace all the qualities that upset us in other people.

1. Refer to your list of words from Exercise 1 in Chapter 4. Sit or stand in front of a mirror and say each word over and over again, "I am [that trait]." Say it until the energy around the word disappears. It works. I have never had people fail this exercise if they are committed to owning a trait. If you get stuck and feel anger or rage at someone who has displayed this trait, or if you feel pissed off that you have this trait, take time out from the mirror and sit down and write a hate letter to this trait. Expressing anger in this way is healthy. These letters are for your eyes only. You are not going to mail them or read them to anyone. You are going to write them as a way to release your built-up emotions. If you don't know what to say, start with, "I am angry at you for . . ." and then write as fast as you possibly can without thinking. Write anything that comes to your mind. Don't worry about grammar or about making sense. Just focus on releasing old emotions and toxicity.

   This exercise is a way of discharging toxic emotions stored in our bodies. If feelings arise during the process, stay with them. You may find it especially difficult to say those words that you have judged harshly. Even if you're crying, stay with the process. At some point you will notice the charge you have on the word releases spontaneously.

2. Using the same list of words, see if you can identify times
in your life when you have demonstrated these traits. If
you cannot think of any time you have exhibited this trait,
then ask yourself in what circumstances might it be
conceivable for you to demonstrate this trait? Would
anyone else say I've demonstrated this trait? Write down
your responses next to each word.

CHAPTER 7

EMBRACING YOUR DARK SIDE

Most of us long to experience peace of mind. This is a life-long pursuit, a task that calls for nothing less than embracing the totality of our being. Discovering the gifts of even our most hated qualities is a creative process that needs only a deep desire to listen and learn, a willingness to release dysfunctional judgments and beliefs, and a readiness to feel better. Your true self makes no judgments. Only our fear-driven egos use judgments to protect us—protection that ironically prevents us from self-realization. We must be prepared to love all that we have feared. "My grievances hide the light of the world," says *A Course in Miracles*.

To get past your ego and its defenses you need to get quiet, be brave, and listen to your inner voices. Behind our social masks lurk thousands of faces. Each face has a personality of its own. Each personality has its own unique characteristics. By having internal dialogues with these sub-personalities you will turn your egotistical prejudices and judgments into priceless treasures. When you embrace the messages of each aspect of your shadow, you begin to take back the power you've given to others and form a bond of trust with your authentic self. The voices of your unembraced qualities, when allowed into your consciousness, will bring you back into balance and harmony with your natural rhythms. They will restore your ability to resolve your own issues and illuminate the purpose of your life. These messages will lead you to discover authentic love and compassion.

Until I started communicating with my sub-personalities I had to rely on others to help me find out what was wrong with me. I went from one therapist to another. I tried local psychics, fortune tellers, and astrologists to get the answers I needed. If I felt there was something wrong with me, if I was feeling angry or sad or even overly happy, I would have to make a call or pay someone to tell me what was going on. What a way to live. If they told me something that I wanted to hear, I would think they were brilliant. But if they told me something I didn't want to hear, I would go to another person, and another, till I got the answer I was seeking.

I knew there had to be a different way to live. Why would God make us so we can't understand ourselves? Why would God make us so we'd have to pay someone else to tell us about ourselves? Now I realize that we're brilliantly designed to heal ourselves and return to wholeness. But sometimes we can use a little help. Talking to our sub-personalities is an excellent exercise to advance the process.

Examining our sub-personalities can be a tool to help us reclaim the lost parts of ourselves. First we must identify these parts and then name them, then we'll be able to disengage from them. Actually naming them creates distance. Roberto Assagioli, founder of psychosynthesis, says that "we are dominated by everything from which our self becomes identified. We can dominate and control everything from which we disidentify ourselves." If I take one of my traits which I don't like, for example *whiney,* and then name it Whiney Wanda, it suddenly seems less threatening to me. In a funny way, as soon as I name these aspects of myself, I feel fondness for them. I can then stand back and look at them in an objective way. This process starts to loosen the grip these behaviors have on your life.

My first experience with sub-personalities was in a transpersonal psychology class at JFK University in Orinda, California. Every week, we would learn and actually experience a different model of emotional healing. The week on psychosynthesis altered my life. I established a dialogue with different aspects of myself which we called sub-personalities and began to find out who they were and what they needed to be whole. The goal was to find their gifts, of course. And in finding each gift, I found acceptance of a disowned part of myself.

Our teacher, Susanne, started with a visualization that took us on an imaginary bus ride. She asked us to see a bus full of people. In my imaginary bus I saw many different kinds of people. Some of them were old, some of them young. They were dressed in everything from miniskirts to bell-bottoms. I saw fat girls, skinny girls, girls with black hair, red hair, big chests and flat chests. I saw every size and shape I could imagine. There were short people, tall people, circus people, people of every color and nationality. There were hookers and saints. It was a big bus, crowded with people, many of whom I didn't want to know. My first thought was, "Oh no, you have to do better than this." Susanne informed us that we'd have to get to know all the people on our bus, the ones we liked as well as the ones we didn't.

Each of these passengers represented an aspect of myself who brought a special gift. They were all there, each offering something unique, if only I would meet them and listen to their wisdom. We were told to let ourselves get off the bus with one of our sub-personalities. And Big Bertha Big Mouth was right there reaching out to take my hand. She was the first sub-personality who wanted to have a conversation with me. When I saw her face I thought, "There is no way I am going for a walk with this woman. I'll find another sub-personality to walk with." Bertha stood about five feet tall, weighed two hundred pounds. She was in her sixties, and was my worst nightmare in terms of appearance. She had thinning gray hair, which was poorly cut and sticking up in front of her face. She reeked of hair spray and cigarettes. She was wearing a beige muumuu with large, orange polka dots. Wrapped around her shoulders was a beige polyester sweater held together by an old, rusty pin. Her legs were fat and her stockings were torn. On her feet were badly worn plastic shoes.

My eyes darted around, looking for someone to save me from Big Bertha. No one came forward. Bertha looked annoyed, and finally just grabbed my hand and dragged me off the bus. We sat down on a nearby bench and Bertha started to talk. She told me she was one of my sub-personalities and I would have to learn to live with her. She said she was not going away and if I would only open my closed mind, I would see that she had a lot to offer. Then Suzanne guided me to ask Big Bertha what she had to teach me. Big Bertha told me I shouldn't judge people by their looks. She said she could see right through my phony spiritual persona. I wanted to argue, but before I began I realized that I had so much prejudice against Big Bertha when I saw her that I didn't even want to talk to her in the privacy of my own mind.

Big Bertha went on to tell me that I'd never get any further in my spiritual development if I didn't deal with this issue. She reminded me that I'd always judged people whom I considered fat and that the only people in my life were those whose external appearances I felt comfortable with. Deep inside I knew Bertha was right. I pretended to be spiritually evolved and not swayed by external things like appearances, but I was lying to myself. I had thought I had ended this behavior years earlier since I had done some work on this issue. But here was Big Bertha, telling me to wake up; there was a lot more work to do. Susanne told us to ask our sub-personalities what their gifts were. Big Bertha said her gift was wholeness. If I really believed I was part of this holographic universe, I would have to accept her whether I liked it or not. She said I would have to look in the eyes of everyone I met with love and compassion to see myself fully. And she told me that meeting her would be one of the most important encounters of my life. She was right.

Big Bertha Big Mouth was a creation of my psyche, based on an aspect of myself I couldn't accept. Through this guided visualization she was able to express herself and teach me a great lesson. It took me months to fully integrate my experience. Everything about her was so real, so pure, so natural. How could this person be part of my subconscious? Where did she come from, how could she be so wise? I kept asking myself these questions. I wanted more of Bertha even though I had been so resistant to accepting her.

Slowly, I gathered the courage to get to the back of my bus and meet some more people. I led myself through the visualization and asked which sub-personality wanted to come out to meet me. In my first encounter alone with this wild group, Angry Alice came out to greet me. She was small and frail with bright red hair that stuck straight up in the air, bushy and teased. Her first words were, "Even though I'm small I'm tough, so don't even think about messing with me." Alice said she was tired of my trying to get rid of her. She told me she was probably the best friend I'd ever have. My anger was there to guide me, and warn me, and when I was in danger Alice screamed in my face. Since I'd always ignored her clues, she had to act out and scream at everyone around me to get my attention. She told me her gift was my strong intuition that would always lead me to healthy relationships. She said the reason I rarely experienced healthy relationships was because I was too busy talking instead of listening to my inner voices.

It was hard to embrace Angry Alice since I'd always believed that I expressed my anger in inappropriate ways. I had been trying for years to get rid of my anger. But Alice didn't need to disappear; she needed acceptance and love. She wanted me to listen to my heart instead of my head. When I started thinking of Alice as my ally she started to calm down. Healthy, sensible expressions of anger took the place of my uncontrollable outbursts.

Next I met Gorging Greta, who liked to eat whole chocolate cakes, and Trashy Trixie, who liked to wear really short skirts and had a foul mouth. Gorging Greta waddled over to tell me she was a close friend of Big Bertha Big Mouth. Her gift was compassion and inner relatedness to all other human beings. She also told me to slow down, and pay attention to myself. Greta said that I'm completely unconscious of how fast I'm running around. I'm a doing machine. And she's the one who freaks out, gorging herself on food in order to feel grounded. Trashy Trixie, on the other hand, came with the gift of grace. She wanted me to treat myself like royalty and behave in a dignified manner. When I didn't she exploded, and had to act out by showing off and being the center of attention. As I explored the positive side of all these negative traits and began to embrace them, they stopped running my life. They were my psyche's great teachers. As soon as I responded to their requests to love them or just to slow down, they became an integrated part of my consciousness and enriched my sense of self-love and wholeness. When I embraced these qualities, it was no longer necessary to eat a whole pint of ice cream or wear skirts that were too short. As soon as I accepted my new friends, they stopped showing up in my life.

I learned this technique when I was living in San Francisco with a man named Rich. We found it was an amusing way to talk about each other's shadows. On a long drive we made a list of each other's sub-personalities that seemed to show up frequently in our relationship. It looked like this:

DEBBIE
Resistant Rita
Angry Alice
Dominating Dixie
Processing Percilla
Princess Paulina
Yolanda the Yogi
Controlling Carrie
Lovergirl Laurie
Righteous Renee

RICH
Dominating Dick
Know-it-all Nick
My-way Marvin
Jimmy the Jock
Loverboy Benny
Competent Ken
Tommy the Teacher

We had a lot of laughs putting together our lists. But we had found a serious way to talk about the parts of each other that seemed to give us the hardest time without creating any upsets in our relationship. When issues came up, I was able to stop pointing my finger at Rich. Instead of saying, "You're trying to dominate me and I don't like it," I was able to say, "It feels like Dominating Dick is out today. Could you talk to him for me?" This automatically drained the tension between us because it never seemed like a personal attack. If I started to process what Rich was saying to me, which I often did, he could just tell Processing Percilla he wasn't in the mood to be processed. I never took this personally, though taking things personally had always been one of my biggest issues in relationships.

Sub-personalities reveal behaviors which we find unacceptable within ourselves. We've shut them out because we couldn't or wouldn't accept them. Because I had closed off certain parts of myself, I was out of touch with the totality of my being. When I looked inside, I discovered these traits were screaming for my attention. And they guided me toward the next step in the transformation of my life. I have come to believe we have as many sub-personalities as we have traits. I have uncovered at least a hundred of my own, and whenever I look I can always find a new face, a new voice, and a new message. Even the darkest sub-personalities come bearing gifts. We just have to be willing to spend some time with each of them in order to hear their voice of wisdom.

You must be willing to spend time exploring your own inner world. In Neale Donald Walsch's *Conversations with God,* God reminds us, "If you do not go within, you go without." If you take this message seriously, it can change your life. When you go within and form a relationship with your entire being you begin to recognize your ability to steer your life in the direction you choose. There is no greater gift you can give yourself. Then when you say, "I want more money, more love, more creativity, more friends, or a healthier body," you will have the faith you need to manifest it.

Trust is always a major issue when you begin a dialogue with your internal voices. The most common question seems to be, "How will I really know if I'm hearing my inner truth?" After a few visits with your sub-personalities it becomes easy to distinguish whether you are talking to a sub-personality or listening to negative chatter. Your negative internal voice will seldom have a positive message or a gift for you. There are many ways to help yourself get to an authentic place within. Meditating can be an ideal way to quiet the mind and its negative inner chatter. If you don't have a regular meditation technique, it may help to buy a meditation tape to give you some direction. Having someone guide you through a series of breathing and body relaxation techniques will help you get out of your head. Another quick and easy thing to try is dance. Put on some beautiful, light music and just let yourself go for a half hour or so. Then sit down, close your eyes, and start to follow your breath. Once you are in a truly quiet place, you'll begin to distinguish your head from your heart. It takes some practice, but once you make this distinction it makes the process of finding and exploring your sub-personalities much easier. Your head can be heartless. Your heart, though it will be straight and tough at times, will always be full of compassion.

It's important to receive your sub-personalities with welcoming arms. Easy to say, but not always easy to do. This is one time when expecting the worst may work in your favor. Then what you get will probably be much better than you thought. People are often shocked by the cast of characters they call up, but that's usually because they were expecting a busload of angels. Sub-personalities might be headless or appear as animals, monsters, or aliens. Whatever you experience in your psyche during a visualization is the right image for you. It's important not to judge whom you meet or what you experience.

It's also common to see people you know—ex-lovers, old bosses, family members. Usually someone you didn't get along with. When these familiar faces show up in your subconscious, resist the urge to blink them away. Stay with them and find out what they're trying to teach you. You may be able to forget about them for now, but if you don't deal with their issues you'll end up meeting them again and again in life. This isn't a card game where you can throw back the sub-personalities you don't want for new ones. In fact, the personalities you least want to see will have the greatest lessons for you.

Recently I worked with a woman who seemed to have it all. Not many women have achieved the level of success, fame, and fortune that Shelly has. She climbed the ladder of success in the entertainment industry and worked very hard to get to the top. She got mostly positive press, but was very sensitive to criticism. After years of going at a pace too fast for most people, Shelly took a few months off to work on herself. She had realized she often acted aggressive but hated this part of herself. When she said, "I am aggressive," her face tightened up and tears came to her eyes. She couldn't live with this aspect of herself. We sat facing each other for a while and I just had her say over and over, "I am aggressive, I am aggressive."

Shelly was still feeling uncomfortable with this aspect of herself, so I had her close her eyes and took her on a bus ride. We called up a sub-personality which she named Aggressive Allie. Allie had big teased red hair and was in her mid fifties. She was dressed in a navy business suit and had a powerful presence. At first Shelly didn't like her. But we asked Aggressive Allie what her gift was to Shelly. Allie said protection. Allie told Shelly that she had protected her while she built her career. Allie said she had made sure no one got in Shelly's way and that no one hurt her or stopped her from attaining her dreams. Then we asked Aggressive Allie what she needed to be whole. Allie wanted love and acceptance. She was tired of being this big, awful, mean woman whom Shelly beat up on. Allie was the person who had made all Shelly's fame and recognition possible. Now she wanted some credit. In her opinion she wasn't asking for a lot from Shelly, only love and appreciation for the part she played in Shelly's life.

Shelly lay on my couch with a huge grin on her face. She was ecstatic. She had fallen in love with Aggressive Alice. She embraced a part of herself that she'd been trying to bury for years. This quality had caused her shame and self-loathing. The paradox was that by not embracing her aggressiveness, Shelly had been robbed of enjoying the gifts of all her success. Shelly was now free to enjoy the fruits of her labor. This is often how it works. You have a quality which has a gift for you. You call on the gift to help get something you want in life. Then because this aspect of yourself is not fully integrated into your psyche and because you've made some negative judgment about it, it takes on a life of its own, acting out in inappropriate ways. Until we embrace the qualities from which we've disassociated ourselves, they will continue to act up until their needs are met. Remember, what you resist persists. When Shelly had accepted Aggressive Allie, her anguish about being aggressive vanished. Now she's free to use this aspect of herself only when and if it's appropriate.

Another useful way to embrace your traits is inviting other people into your consciousness to get their perspective on disowned aspects. Visualize someone you admire and respect, perhaps someone who is holy or spiritual. Now concentrate on one of the words that you still find hard to embrace. Ask the person you've chosen how they would interpret this aspect of yourself. Make sure you pick someone who is wise and compassionate. Or try it with someone important from your past, preferably a parent or family member. Here's an example from my own life:

My word is "sloppy." Since I don't approve of this part of myself I try to hide it from the world. I orchestrate my life so that I have a nanny who takes care of my son and cleans my house. She keeps everything clean and in perfect order. Even though I'm not the one who keeps my surroundings impeccable, this is the way I like my home to look. No one ever calls me sloppy because my home is always neat and clean. But if someone said Debbie Ford is a slob it would *affect* me. So I close my eyes, take some slow, deep breaths, and think about the word sloppy. It makes me feel a little sick and tight. Underneath that is the feeling of fear. I trace the feeling into my past and remember my mother yelling at me for being sloppy. I was afraid I wouldn't be loved if I was a sloppy person. With my eyes closed I picture Mother Teresa in my heart and I ask her how I could reinterpret the word so I am no longer hateful of sloppy. I say to her that I want to put love on this word and then I allow myself to hear her voice. She replies by telling me my sloppiness is play. It's the way I express the child in me. Throwing clothes on the floor is fun for me and I can stop making it wrong. She tells me the gift of sloppiness is order. Because I grew up always being reminded what a slob I was I now have a unique ability to organize everything and have it look perfect. Now I have one new powerful interpretation.

Then I close my eyes again and I ask Martin Luther King, Jr., to give me a new interpretation for my sloppiness. I picture him in my heart and he says that because I have so much passion for life I have an urgency to go on to the next thing. This shows up as my sloppiness. I'm too excited to tend to the little things, like putting things back where they belong. He says my passion and enthusiasm are the gifts of my sloppiness. By taking responsibility for my sloppiness and hiring someone to take care of those things that I don't like to do, I can take care of more important business. Interpretation Two.

Now I'm starting to love my sloppiness. Feeling brave, I visualize my mother who always criticized my sloppiness. I ask her for a new powerful interpretation. She says, "The reason I always criticized you for being sloppy was because I was jealous that I never had the internal freedom to just throw a piece of clothing on the floor and leave it there." She said she was always rigid with herself, even as a child, and couldn't stand anything out of place. My sloppiness was a reminder of her rigidity. That's why it upset her so much. She went on to tell me my sloppiness gave me the gift of self-expression. When I was young I loved to paint. I just dove in and tried different colors and strokes, sometimes I used my hands. I was never afraid to try something for fear of making a mess. My sloppiness gave me freedom. Interpretation Three.

I could go on, but in fewer than ten minutes I had a new respect for my sloppiness. Now it feels like a loving, positive characteristic that has given me many gifts. I can really see that I was just having fun and expressing myself. Now when I close my eyes and think about the word sloppy I feel open and receptive. Love heals, and it's sometimes just a matter of inventing a new interpretation of a feeling or an experience.

As you go about embracing your disowned traits, it can be useful to retrace the steps that led you to believe that a certain quality was bad in the first place. Going back to the time when a characteristic began to have power over you enables you to expose the origin of your ego-driven judgment. My friend Peter was having trouble embracing his weakness. So I asked him to close his eyes and find an image from his past that exemplified his weakness. His first memory was of high school, when he chose a different sport every season because he felt inadequate and uncompetitive. He recalled feeling weak among his classmates at an all-boys' private school. I asked Peter to go deeper and find an even earlier incident. Then Peter remembered a time when he was eight years old. He was visiting the site where his family was building their new home. The stairs leading to the second level had no backs, so you could see through them to the floor below. Peter remembered his mother and sister leading him up to see his new room. But when Peter was ready to leave, his mom and sister had already gone back down the stairs. He was afraid to climb down alone for fear he might slip through the holes in the steps. Seeing his mother and sister on the first floor, he called to them but they refused to help. His mother told him he'd have to do it alone, or they'd leave him behind. Paralyzed by fear, Peter stayed put. His mother and sister left and didn't return for half an hour. At that point he internalized the lesson, "If I'm weak, women will leave me." Since then, Peter couldn't be weak because he believed it would cause women who love him to leave.

Most of us are driven by the eight-year-old within us. That child who didn't get his needs met is begging for acceptance. So it's useful to delve into your memory as far back as possible. From that place that you can more easily find compassion for an aspect of yourself. Peter was a tough guy for years, and his relationships with women never lasted more than six months. He always left them. By retracing his disowned weakness, Peter was able to find the origin of its power. By facing this early incident he was able to own his weakness. To help him embrace this aspect, I asked Peter to choose two people he admired who had an abundance of compassion and humanity. He chose the Buddha and the Dalai Lama. Bringing the Buddha forth in his mind, Peter asked what the gift of his weakness was. The Buddha responded by saying it gave Peter a deep compassion for other people's weaknesses. From the Dalai Lama, Peter learned that his weakness was the source of his dynamic personality and his ability to make other people comfortable in social situations. Feeling weak provided him with a strong desire to develop a loving and engaging external persona.

Then I asked Peter to think of one of his parents. With his eyes closed, he brought his father into his consciousness. His father told him that by always having to overcome his weakness Peter learned to be resilient and bounce back from all kinds of situations. Because Peter couldn't accept his weakness he had always taken the hard road to prove how strong he was. He needed to show the world his strength by creating a life full of mishaps, wrong turns, and missed opportunities. Peter's father predicted that if he started to learn these lessons and embraced his weakness, he would start manifesting the easy road.

Recently, I learned that Peter is writing music, a passion of his which he never thought would be a viable career path. Instead of starting a new job and a new relationship every six months, Peter is channeling his energy into writing songs and producing a demo tape of his work. He is learning to create a world without suffering. A world where it's safe to express his emotions and his creativity.

If we don't shift our perceptions of our true selves, we'll be stuck repeating our past behaviors. Your sub-personalities can tell you what work is left unfinished, what you have to do to resolve reoccurring patterns. They will tell you what you need to do to learn a specific lesson. If you're willing to listen you will find your sub-personalities are funny, resourceful, honest, and forgiving—the wisest people in the universe when it comes to yourself. This is because they're giving you answers that come from within you.

You can access anybody you know by going within. All you have to do is get quiet and call forth that person in your subconscious. And when you visualize a particular person and start a dialogue with him you can ask anything you want. You can ask what he thinks about a particular issue and what advice there is for you. Everyone's voice can be found inside of you—the answers you need from all the people can come from within. All your unresolved relationships and all your lovers, family members and friends, and heroes and gurus. All the people you have shut out or have shut you out. Each one of these people can speak to you and speak through you.

A couple of years ago, I was having a difficult time trying to decide what I wanted to do with my life. During this period I closed my eyes and asked myself, "Whom should I go to for some advice?" There was a man I'd gotten to know years earlier whom I respected tremendously. My friend Steve's face appeared to me. For days I went back and forth in my mind trying to decide if I should bother him. It seemed somewhat inappropriate to call him about my career decisions and boyfriend problems. We weren't really friends anymore. One day during my meditation I attempted to visualize Steve and ask him what he thought I should do. I'd never tried this before, but I knew I had nothing to lose. The most astonishing thing happened: Steve started talking to me. He told me he was glad I'd come to him for help, and he answered all of my questions, clearly and concisely. When I finished it felt like I'd just spent an hour with the real Steve, receiving his wisdom and feeling his love. It was an amazing, eye-opening experience—simple, direct, and to the point. I didn't even have to leave my house or spend money on a phone call! For months I called on the Steve within me to guide me on my path. I'd found a friend and confidant within myself.

My girlfriend Sirah used a similar technique with me after my father passed away. I went to see her in the middle of my grieving, when I was feeling particularly sad that my father would never get to know my son, Beau. Sirah had me close my eyes and visualize my father playing with my son. It was as though my father was standing right in front of me telling Beau he'd always be there to protect him. My father told Beau how much he himself loved music and hoped Beau would also find joy and beauty in music and play one of the instruments he had left behind. This was a moving and extremely valuable experience. It changed the way I felt about the loss of my father. When I left the session with Sirah I was sure my father would always be there to guide and comfort me and that I could bring him close to Beau by sharing his love of music with Beau. The feeling of loss shifted from a hopeless, sinking feeling of despair to one of optimism.

Your sub-personalities are there waiting for you—go in and reclaim them. They want nothing more than attention and acceptance. They are the voices of your future, not your past. They will always be there to guide you, embrace you, and comfort you, whether they come in the form of someone you know or in the form of some shadowy figure. If you befriend yourself, you'll break the continuing cycle of loss of self or loss of others. What you'll find out is that we never lose anyone: our relationships simply change form. Someone might not be there physically, but will always be there, within us. By reclaiming everything you hate about yourself, you open up a world within where you have access to the entire universe.

We each have the capacity to give ourselves everything we

need to be happy and whole. When we reconnect with our whole selves, it's virtually impossible to feel lonely, isolated, or left out. We need to find the universe within us, and learn how to love, honor, and respect that universe. Then we can accept the magnitude of ourselves. When we discover the magic of the world within, we stand in awe of ourselves. With that awe comes peace, satisfaction, and gratitude for our humanity.

Every single sub-personality has a gift for you. Every aspect of you, whether you like it or not, can benefit your life. To think there is only darkness is to deceive yourself. There is light in every part of us and every part of the universe. To not find our gifts is to reject the extraordinary design of life. Our souls long to learn these valuable lessons. We need to stop judging our souls' journey and trust in the design of our humanity and eternal goodness. There is an ancient saying, "All things must grow, or they die." Our highest purpose is to learn and grow from our experiences and then move on. Once we receive the benefit of our traits we are free to choose the experiences we desire.

EXERCISE

Do this exercise when you are very relaxed, after a walk or a bath. You are going to meet your inner voices so you want to have your mind as quiet as possible. Early in the morning or before you go to bed is also a good time. Put on some soft music and light an aromatherapy candle to help you create a relaxed mood. Close your eyes and start following your breath. Take long, slow, deep breaths, retaining the breath for five or more seconds, and then slowly exhale. Do this four or five times until your mind is quiet.

Now imagine stepping onto a large, yellow bus. Take a seat in the middle of the bus. You're feeling excited about taking a long-awaited trip. Imagine riding down the street on a clear, beautiful day. You're sitting there minding your own business when someone taps you on your shoulder. You look up and this person says, "Hello, I'm one of your sub-personalities and all the other people on this bus are also your sub-personalities. Why don't you get up now and walk around and see who's on your bus." You get up from your seat and you walk through the entire bus looking at all the different people in their seats . . .

You see before you every kind of person—tall people, short people, teenagers, and old people. There might be circus people, animals, and homeless people. With you on the bus are people of every race, color, and creed. Some of them are waving to get your attention, others may be hiding quietly in the corner. Continue to walk through the aisles, slowly visualizing all the characters on the bus. Now the bus driver directs you to allow one of your sub-personalities to take you for a walk off the bus in a nearby park. Take your time and allow one of your sub-personalities to come and take your hand, and escort you off the bus into the park.

Sit down next to this person and ask his or her name. Ask that person to tell you what trait he or she represents along with a name. For example, if you meet someone angry you could name this person Angry Alfred or Angry Ann. If you don't hear a name you give that person one. Take all the time you need. Notice how this person is dressed and looks. What does this person smell like? Notice his or her mood and body language. Take another deep breath and ask, "What is your gift to me?" After you have received the gift, ask, "What do you need to be whole?" Or "What do you need to integrate into my psyche?"

After you have heard every answer ask this person, "Is there anything else you need to say to me?" When you are finished make sure you acknowledge and walk this person back to the bus. When you are ready, open your eyes and write down the messages you received from your sub-personality. Then take out your journal and write for at least ten minutes about your experience.

Don't worry if you did not get all the answers you needed from your sub-personality. It takes time and practice to hear all of their messages. Make a date with yourself to do it again. This is an exercise that requires you to surrender to yourself, so make sure you have created a safe environment for the process.

CHAPTER 8

REINTERPRETING
YOURSELF

When left unhealed, the past will destroy our lives. It buries our unique gifts, our creativity, and our talents. And when these parts of ourselves go unclaimed they stagnate inside us: we use them against our world instead of in harmony with it. We think we're mad at the world, that we want to change the world, that if only the world were different we'd be able to live our dreams. But it's we who need to change. We're angry at ourselves for not persisting, for not honoring the god force inside us, for not giving ourselves permission to express ourselves as we truly desire. We think we're mad at our parents for repressing us early in life. Actually we're angry at ourselves for perpetuating that repression. It's as if, a long time ago, someone put us in a cage and although the cage hasn't been there for years we still struggle against its imaginary walls. The cage is our self-imposed limitations, our self-doubt, and our fear. We were taught that it's hard work to go after our dreams. We may not have understood that it's even more difficult living day in and day out with the knowledge that we don't pursue them. We are left without desire, which is the key to fulfilling our full spiritual potential. We are left with desperation, which builds up slowly and expresses itself in our bodies as disease and in our psyche as rage. If we're unwilling to make peace with the past, we'll simply drag our desperation and rage into the future.

The strength to look clearly at your past and take back aspects of yourself that you've given away lies within you. All you have to do is close your eyes, go within, and ask. The power you need is there, but it will only come out when your desire to change your life is stronger than your desire to stay the same. It's always easier to blame others for the condition of our lives. When we lose touch with ourselves we lose touch with our divinity, and because we don't trust ourselves we come to believe that other people can't be trusted. For some people the pain of the past is so great they believe the only way they can cope with it is to blame and deny. You must embrace your past if you want to change your present. If you want to manifest your desires you must be accountable for everything that takes place in your world.

If you want to see someone's future, often all you have to do is look at their past. The past leads us to conclude that all we can hope for in the future is a variation on what we already have. This stops most people in their tracks. It clouds their vision and lets their dreams slip away. Look around and you'll see that most people stay the same. You could look at their lives now, and then again in twenty years, when you would see only a slight variation on the original theme. Our core issues, whether they are based on sex, wealth, relationships, health, or career, often remain dominant throughout our lives. Our past shapes what we say, what we see, and how we live. Some of us are not only dragging our own past around, but those of our parents as well. Pain is passed down from generation to generation, and if it's not questioned, we'll never break the cycle.

We begin to disown parts of ourselves because of our core beliefs, which are always tied to our families and early childhood. What our parents did and didn't do had great impact on our lives. Our caregivers and teachers also contributed to who we are now. The pain you experienced when you were two, six, or eight is just beneath the surface of your consciousness. Until it's transformed, it's always there driving your life. Most of us never explore our core beliefs to see if we've consciously chosen them. I meet people every week who want to be artists or write books, but they are sure they can't fulfill their desires. When I ask them why, they tell me they're not talented or educated enough. They have confidence in their reasons, but not in their dreams. And when we explore the origins of their beliefs, we learn that most often they've been told by someone they love, verbally or non-verbally, that they weren't capable of fulfilling their dreams. Since they never questioned this idea, they're trapped by it. They never even try to attain their heart's desire.

Core beliefs that run our lives sound like this, "I can't do it. It will never happen to me. I'm not deserving. I'm not good enough." Recently a young woman whose name was Hallie came to one of my courses. She was twenty-one years old. Because she suffered from depression and wasn't able to take care of herself, she lived at home with her mother. When the course began Hallie sat quietly, looking down, avoiding eye contact with everyone. She had a nervous habit of tapping her hand on the table, which was distracting to anyone sitting near her. During rest breaks Hallie could often be found on the ground in fetal position. I asked everyone to eat meals with someone else, but Hallie sat alone. On the second day, I walked by Hallie and asked her if she had owned "poor me." She looked at me with a puzzled smile and asked, "Me?" I couldn't help laughing. Hallie's silent message was so loud it was screaming at us. I sat down next to her and asked her what she thought she was communicating to the world. Hallie said she didn't think of herself as a "poor me." In fact, she hated "poor me" people, her mother being one of them. When my assistant Rachel and I pointed out Hallie's behaviors to her the entire puzzle of her life seemed to fall into place. Hallie told us that deep inside she believed she was unlovable. "Poor me" was a way of getting attention. Since she had grown up in a home where her mother acted like a child, even spoke like a child, Hallie had learned to outdo her mother for attention.

This core belief that she was unlovable was well hidden from Hallie because she had projected it onto her mother. She couldn't see herself clearly. All her energy was devoted to believing she wasn't like her mother. But when we showed her how she appeared to us, Hallie realized her behavior was a direct result of observing her mother. By embracing "poor me" and becoming conscious of her little girl act, Hallie allowed the opposites of these traits to surface. What developed in her was, "I'm a responsible woman." And within a few months, Hallie got a job and moved out of her mother's house into her own apartment. Feeling confident, Hallie met a man and began an intimate relationship for the first time in years. As soon as Hallie was willing to see the core belief that was driving her, and to examine it honestly, she gained the freedom to choose a new path for her life.

We adopt many beliefs unconsciously from our families, and the rest of the life choices we make are colored by these beliefs without our ever asking, "Does this belief empower me?" We're often just following in the footsteps of our family members. This is fine if the reality you adopt is making you happy, but if it's not, question it. Prejudice is passed down. Pain is passed down. Guilt is passed down. Shame is passed down. Are your problems your own or have you inherited them from former generations?

My grandmother is a chronic worrier. Her core belief is, "Something bad is about to happen." My mother doesn't worry at all, but I adopted my grandmother's worrying. I often have the same types of thoughts that she has. We mirror each other's worries about the safety of my son. As obvious as it seems now, it took me years to realize that I adopted this trait from my grandmother who adopted it from her father. When I find myself worrying now, I have to stop and ask myself whether I'm really worried or am I just acting out one of my old core beliefs. As soon as I identify that I have nothing to worry about and acknowledge being stuck in a family pattern I can affirm my own truth. Every time I break up my automatic responses by looking closely at myself, I elevate my consciousness. Then I can shake free of my past.

Many people have decided that they *will not* be like their parents. But we all must acknowledge that we've spent years absorbing our parents' positive and negative qualities. Our parents did the best they could given their own pasts. We cannot change the way we were raised, and when we're willing to look for the lessons in our experiences, we'll be able to see that each incident provided us with an opportunity to learn and grow. One of my best friends, who was sexually molested by her grandfather for years, once said to me, "Thank God for all the abuse of my past because I have become one of the most resourceful people on the planet. I got here by learning how to deal with all the pain and abuse of my past."

All negative events are blessings in disguise. Some of us choose to live under the illusion that bad things happen for no good reason. But pain has a purpose. It teaches us and guides us to higher levels of awareness. One night, while I was meditating after seeing five or six young men being arrested and handcuffed at the beach, I asked God, "Why, on this glorious summer night, did these boys have to start a fire at the beach?" A voice within me said this was Spirit guiding these young men back home. Getting in trouble was a wake-up call from the God force inside them. In prisons you'll often see hundreds of tough young men reading Bibles and attending religious services. Men who'd never spent so much as an hour of their adult lives thinking about God are now searching their souls for answers. The challenges in our lives can provide insights which help us free ourselves from a past which strangles our passion and keeps us from our spiritual center.

An ancient teaching says, "The world is a teacher to the wise man and an enemy to the fool." No event is painful in and of itself. It's all a matter of perspective. It's important to understand that everything happening in the world is as it should be at every moment. There are no mistakes. There are no accidents. The world is a heavenly sky and a bottomless pit. When we understand that we cannot have one without the other, it becomes easier to accept the world as it is. I look back at my own past filled with lies and deceit, hurt and pain, drugs and sex. But I see that without all these experiences and without all the darkness I carried around for so long, I wouldn't be able to teach as I do today. Every incident from my past, every sleepless night, every tear carries me a little closer to fulfilling my soul's journey. No one says what I say in the way I say it. No one does the things I do in the exact way I do them. I am me and you are you. Each of us is unique and we all have a special journey of our own.

I was thirteen when my parents divorced. This event upset me emotionally for many years. During holidays I became sad and depressed, wishing the New Year would come soon so things could get back to normal. Then one evening I had a specific insight into why I felt so bad. I always spent those holidays with my mother, and it occurred to me that the thought of my father being without his children on Thanksgiving was upsetting me. And what was more upsetting was my being without my father.

I stayed in my sullen mood, knowing there was nothing I could do about the situation. Feeling unworthy and powerless, I declared the past complete. I said out loud, "I did this." I created this so I could grow and if I don't like the reality that is in front of me I'd have to create a different one. I started imagining different scenarios. Going to my father's for an early dinner and then to my mother's for a late one. I imagined just going to see my father and not my mother. All these scenarios also seemed depressing but then I got an idea. I called my mother who always hosted Thanksgiving dinner and suggested that I host it this year. Enthusiastically she said it sounded like a great idea. Then I quietly suggested that I'd like to invite my father and his family. I told her it would mean so much to me to have everyone together. At first there was silence. I thought the line had gone dead until I heard my mother say, "If that's what you'd like, go right ahead."

Joyfully I called my dad and invited him and his entire family to my house for Thanksgiving. He was surprised and asked me what my mother was going to do. I told him she would be coming with her entire family too. He agreed and there it was. In moments I had created a situation I had never thought possible. When I called my sister and brother and told them everyone was coming to my house for Thanksgiving they were shocked and skeptical, but everyone came. The event was a success. I invited some of my friends and their families to ease the stress and set up big long tables to accommodate everyone. Thirty-three people came, everyone brought their favorite dish and everyone brought a genuine holiday spirit. For the next three years, until I sold my house and moved out west, I hosted these holiday dinners which included both sides of my family. By taking responsibility I was able to see a new reality emerge, a reality that even to this day seems like a miracle.

In order to gain wisdom and freedom from your past, you must take responsibility for all the events that have happened in your life. Taking responsibility means being able to say to yourself, "I did that." There's a big difference between the world doing things to you and your doing things to yourself. When you take responsibility for the events in your life and for your interpretation of those events, you step out of the world of a child and into the world of an adult. By claiming responsibility for your action and your inaction, you give up the story line of "Why me?" and turn it into "This happened to me because I needed to learn a lesson. This is part of my journey."

According to Nietzsche, to wish away our past is to wish ourselves out of existence. It's nearly impossible to steer our lives in a particular direction until we come to terms with our past. Each significant event in our lives changes how we view the world and ourselves. The thought of reviewing our entire past is often overwhelming. But it's an essential part of the process. Our past is a blessing that guides and teaches, and it carries as many positive messages as it does negative.

A friend called me one day to complain about her life. Every time Nancy looked in the mirror she saw her body getting softer and her face looking more like her mother's. She said she could see all the stress, worry, and disappointments being etched into her face. Nancy asked me what she could do to deal with her hot flashes and her sad, falling face. She said she realized she was gaining weight in order to look pregnant as a way to reclaim her lost youth. Together Nancy and I designed a program for her to journal, meditate, and do anger-release work every day for twenty-eight days. She needed to complete her past and to release all her stored emotions. Nancy willingly opened herself up and batted while focusing on the words old, fat, pathetic, and ugly: the words that she didn't want to be. After twenty-eight days of doing this release, Nancy felt complete. Different issues came up for her along the way, so she took whatever time she needed to journal and invent new interpretations for each event. It was a long month but at the end she felt totally ready to love and nurture herself.

The next twenty-eight days Nancy spent loving every part of who she was. She told me she needed to be hugged and kissed, so she hugged and kissed herself. She forgave herself completely. Finally she was at peace. Recently Nancy called me to tell me she had decided to have a face-lift. She said having embraced "old" she could now embrace "young" at a whole new level. She wanted to know if I thought she was still running away from "old." We chatted for a while and it was clear Nancy didn't need the surgery, but it was a decision that would empower her in her personal life and in her job. Nancy is an esthetician and makeup artist. I explained that many people love themselves the way they are but choose to shave their underarms or wax the hair above their lips. We do these things to look better and there's nothing wrong with it as long as we're the ones choosing and as long as we're not running away from ourselves.

Nancy explained that it had all fallen into place like a miracle. One day at a plastic surgeon's office where she worked part-time the nurses asked her if she would like to create a fantasy face on the computer. Nancy thought it might be fun. The new image of Nancy turned her on, but still she had never thought seriously about having her face done. Months later, Nancy mentioned the experience to her husband. Without even being asked he told her if she wanted to have a face-lift he'd pay for it. Nancy said the moment just fell into place. Nancy had the surgery and loves the results. She said it wasn't until she felt good about who she was that she could even think about having plastic surgery. Nancy's pain had guided her to do inner work. By transforming her inner self she was able to transform her outer self.

Our pain can be our greatest teacher. It leads us to places we'd never go on our own. How many people would choose to spend twenty years in pain so that they could find and fulfill their soul's journey? If I hadn't been in so much pain, I might still be stoned, sunbathing on the deck of a race boat in Miami Beach, talking about myself. The positive and the negative got me where I am today. Would I choose to go through all the pain again to have what I have now? The answer is yes! I bless my past and my pain. But before I embraced my darkness I hated it. I resented pain, and I resented others who seemed to live without it. It took me a long time to accept responsibility for my actions. I had tried so hard not to take responsibility for anything. It wasn't until I was ready to look at a higher version of my life that I realized God was trying to teach me something and that I had a special gift which I would find only if I went through the darkness. Today I strive to take full responsibility for every incident in my past to learn what was necessary to get me where I needed to go.

Taking responsibility is a huge task. Most of us are willing to take responsibility for the good we create in our lives, but we often resist taking responsibility for the bad. When we take responsibility, we can be empowered by everything. Even if we feel hurt or ashamed by something that happens, we can find peace in the knowledge that somehow it's helping each of us to fulfill our dreams or direct our soul's journey. We can look at ourselves and say, "the world is my canvas and I drew this event into my life to teach myself a valuable lesson." We become accountable for everything that happens. We say to the universe, "I am the source of my own reality." This is the place of power from which you can alter your life.

Until you look the past directly in the eye it will always be there, bringing more of the same into your life. Psychologist Rollo May defined insanity as "doing the same thing over and over again expecting different results." We must learn from our past and reclaim the parts of ourselves we have disowned. This is how we can break the cycle. Those who have learned from a bad experience, taken responsibility for their feelings, and made a conscious commitment to have their life be different will seldom create the same situation again. If we approach our lives with awareness we can begin to make new and different decisions about what we want to create. A shift in perception is all we need.

To alter our perception we must search each moment in our past until we find a powerful interpretation that allows us to take responsibility. We waste valuable energy creating reasons for why things aren't our fault. It's always easier to blame someone else for what we don't like about our world, but that path is a dead end. There's always pain when you are a victim of circumstance: the pain of desperation and powerlessness. But you live in a universe where everything happens for a reason. Find a blessing for all the events that have taken place in your life and you will find gratitude. You will experience what it's like to be blessed.

Every word, incident, and person that still has an emotional charge needs to be *retraced, faced, replaced, and embraced*. We need to retrace our steps back to the genesis of the emotional charge. Then we face the incident, owning up to its reality as part of our past. We need to become fully aware of the influence it has had on our life. Then we look at the incident from a different perspective which allows us to replace our negative feelings with positive ones. We take control of our lives by choosing our interpretations. That enables us to embrace our disowned past and unplug ourselves from other people.

We must choose interpretations that move our lives forward rather than leave us feeling alone and helpless. It's my belief that inventing a new interpretation is the simplest way to transform something negative into something positive. Everything that occurs in our world is an objective event. It has no inherent meaning. Each of us sees the world through different lenses, so each of us will perceive a particular incident differently. It's our perceptions and our interpretations that affect our emotions not the incident itself. It's our perceptions and interpretations that deny responsibility and lay blame. Whom do you blame for your selfishness? Your addictions? Your failures? Now is the time to stop being a victim. Accept responsibility and you will accept your selfishness, addictions, and failures. You will also unleash your generosity, your grace, and your divine right to have it all. Each of us has to come to terms with how we're affected by holding on to an old, unevolved view of ourselves and our lives. Each of us has to make a conscious decision to alter our world by altering our interpretations. Shift your interpretation of a word, and not only will it lose its negative charge, it will return your own power to you.

Here is an exercise that will help you alter your interpretations. I will take a word that has an emotional charge, which I still don't want to be called. The word I want to create a new interpretation for is "ugly." I go back through my memories and find an early incident in my life that caused me pain and formed my judgments about ugliness. When I *retrace*, I remember my father used to tease me by calling me "pignose" and "bucky" when I was a little girl. My interpretation: my father doesn't love me and thinks I'm ugly. I know this feeling has haunted me, so now I must choose to *face* the incident. I allow myself to experience the feelings of pain, humiliation, and shame I still attach to that moment and to that word. Then I begin to create a new interpretation of the event in order to embrace "ugly."

NEW INTERPRETATIONS

Positive

1. I am beautiful, so my father became nervous around me. The only way he knew how to deal with his nervousness was by calling me names that he thought were cute.

2. My father thought these names were cute and used them with affection.

3. My father loved me so much that he wanted to prepare me for the real world. He thought he could protect me by downplaying my beauty.

Negative

1. My father hated me and was trying to damage me for life.

2. My father thought I truly was remarkably ugly and the only way he could deal with it was by teasing me.

Now I can look at all the interpretations and see which ones make me feel good and which ones make me feel bad. And I can choose to replace my old negative interpretation with a new positive interpretation. I always ask myself, "Does this interpretation empower me or disempower me? Does this interpretation make me feel weak or strong?" If you have an inner dialogue that disempowers you, it won't change until you yourself replace it with a positive, powerful, internal conversation. But some of us are very strong-willed, and our addiction to pain and suffering won't allow a new interpretation. This is why it's so important to write things out and look at every single way you might perceive a particular incident. Just the act of writing down the words shakes loose the emotions that are tied to the incident. When we're willing to have some fun and play with our interpretations we can re-examine our choices. When we bring them out of the darkness and into the light, they can be healed.

The new interpretation I chose in this instance was that "My father loved me so much he wanted to prepare me for the real world. He thought by downplaying my beauty he could protect me." I picked it because it made me laugh. It seemed a little ridiculous when I wrote it down, but when I closed my eyes and asked myself which interpretation nurtured my soul, it was this one. Once I chose to replace the old interpretation I was able to embrace "ugly" without feeling past pain. Now my internal reference point has shifted. Now my father's old habit seems almost light and sweet. Regardless of his true motives, I'm now at peace with that experience. I no longer walk around fearing that someone will think I'm ugly. Nor do I project the ugliness I felt about myself onto other people. The gift of ugly is the freedom to walk out of my house without combing my hair or putting on makeup and still feel great.

You can use the exercise we just did with any incident or word you are having problems with, however trivial or intense. A woman I worked with was understandably having great difficulty finding any blessing in the fact that she had been held at gunpoint and raped. She took from the experience a feeling that she was a disgusting, sleazy whore and deserved it. She had carried this interpretation around for more than fifteen years. I asked her to try to invent three positive interpretations and two more negative interpretations. She could see clearly that the one she had chosen was disempowering and painful. So she invented the negative ones first.

Negative
1. Because I was a rebel and hated my parents, I dressed provocatively and I got what I deserved.
2. I am a low-life scum who has no value. I deserve to be used and abused.

Positive
1. I was a lost and naive young girl just trying to belong. This event helped guide me toward becoming a more conscious, careful, aware person.
2. This incident was a blessing in disguise. As a result of it I learned how to respect myself and respect my body.
3. I learned I never had to be a victim again. This incident was a wake-up call, part of a divine plan to awaken my spiritual self.

Once Hannah had come up with all these interpretations, she realized that she had a choice. We had gone through the negative interpretations first because Hannah had thought it would be impossible to invent positive ones. But by the time we had finished, Hannah was able to find many different interpretations that could empower her. She even admitted that the one she chose felt like the truth. She chose the second of the positive statements above: *This incident was a blessing in disguise. As a result of it I learned how to respect myself and respect my body.* As soon as Hannah made the decision to alter her interpretation she was able to embrace "sleazy" and "disgusting," two words that had run her life for over fifteen years. By allowing these aspects to present her with their gifts she also made room for their polar opposites to emerge. Proud and beautiful were what Hannah longed to be, and now she had access to these integral parts of herself.

As you become more conscious it will be increasingly evident that it's your responsibility to choose empowering interpretations. It is sometimes easier to be a victim, but a negative perspective provides you with a guarantee of more of the same. The more aware you are of the gifts of life the faster you will choose your own perspective on everything that happens to you. Tragic events happen to many of us. It's a part of life. It takes courage to empower yourself through these events. But when you use these times to grow they become blessings.

Another courageous example is the life of a beautiful young woman named Julia. Julia had desperately wanted a child for a couple of years. When she finally became pregnant, she and her husband were ecstatic. Around the fourteenth week of her pregnancy, Julia noticed she was bleeding. Frightened, she immediately went to see her midwife. When they couldn't find a heartbeat, she went in for a sonogram. Again, no heartbeat—the baby was dead. Julia was devastated. She cried for days, mourning her loss. While the dead fetus was still inside her I was privileged to do some work with Julia. I asked for her interpretation of this tragic event. Julia began to cry. She said, "I'm not good enough to give birth to a child. It must have been the alcohol I drank before I knew I was pregnant that damaged my baby."

To the natural pain of her grief, Julia was adding the blame she placed on herself. As we spoke, it became clear to me that Julia wanted to make this a sacred event, not just another bad thing that had happened to her. When we began our work, Julia wanted to create the negative interpretations first.

Negative
1. I'll never be able to carry a child full-term because I'm genetically defective.
2. I'm being punished for all the abortions of my friends and family.

Positive
1. This is a practice run for my body, preparing the way for the baby I will love and nurture.
2. This confirms that my desire to have a baby is real. I no longer feel any ambivalence.
3. The pain of loss and separation gave me experience that will help me be a better mother.

Julia choose to embrace the third positive statement: *The pain of loss and separation gave me experience that will help me be a better mother.* She could feel the power of this interpretation in her body. Knowing there are no accidents, Julia wanted to remember this child for the gift that it brought her rather than the pain. This was truly an act of love and courage. It empowered Julia to go on with her life and get ready for the beautiful child she would eventually mother.

Each of us must trust that if we do what is necessary to clear out the past and embrace our pain, we'll find our unique gifts, the gold in the dark. If we allow it, the universe will give us more than we can possibly imagine. We each come into this world with a different mission, and it's up to us to play that out. From this perspective you'll see that all the events in your past provide an opportunity to learn, grow, change, and explore.

When we're reconciled with our past, the process of taking back our projections becomes much easier. These disowned emotions and behaviors are giving away our power and our capacity to be great. When you deny a single aspect of yourself, you're denying a part of what you need to be whole. We give away our most treasured aspects to those we hate and those we love without knowing it. We can't embrace certain things because we have so much invested in our judgments and criticisms. We lack the courage to be wrong, to be responsible. We're afraid of being imperfect, of realizing that the things we hate most about others are really just the things we hate about ourselves. We are afraid that our power and our brilliance will isolate us because all we see around us is mediocrity. We are so fearful of being rejected that we sell out our most precious gifts just to fit in. We're taught this as a means of survival, and we do it until we can't stand ourselves anymore. Then the toxic emotions become so painful that we create situations in our lives to continually show us we're unworthy, to prove we're not deserving of our dreams. Only you can stop the vicious circle. Only you can say, "No more. I want my greatness. I deserve my brilliance, my creativity, and my divinity."

For years I experienced a painful lack of trust with all of my intimate partners. I believed that men could not be trusted and if given the chance would be unfaithful. It never occurred to me that this might have anything to do with me. So I kept constant track of my boyfriends, threatening to end our relationship if they did anything to break our exclusive bond. Finally, one man suggested that I was projecting my own lack of trustworthiness onto him. I immediately rejected the idea. I was certainly loyal and trustworthy. Later, after we'd had an argument, I noticed the first thing I did was think about the next man I'd have a relationship with, my next Mr. Right. We hadn't even discussed breaking off our relationship and here I was having a fantasy about another man. But because I told myself it was only a fantasy, I was able to deny this part of myself. As soon as I could acknowledge my own untrustworthiness I was able to stop projecting that lack of trust onto those around me.

Discovering that I was the one creating turmoil in my relationships was very upsetting. My first response was loathing for what I perceived as a sick part of myself. I closed my eyes to see if I could talk to my untrustworthy sub-personality. The first image that came to me was that of a small, frail girl who trembled at the sight of men. Her name was Scared Sue. When I asked her what she needed to be healed, she said compassion. Hearing these words and seeing her fear opened up my heart. I allowed myself to feel my own fear, and with my eyes closed I held Scared Sue in my arms. Compassion for ourselves is essential. Where it is absent, we feel fear and self-loathing. Since it's unbearable to hate ourselves, we project that hatred onto the world. We'd rather be victims of the world than victims of ourselves, and by blaming the world we can avoid the pain of facing ourselves.

Now is the time to look honestly at everyone in your life to whom you react strongly—your mother, father, partner, boss, or best friend. Make a list of who they are and which of their qualities trigger a reaction. This is a process of continual discovery. Once you own one layer of traits another layer will expose itself. Any resentments you hold are red flags, signaling that you're still energetically plugged in.

In her book *A Course in Love,* Joan Gattuso illustrates an easy exercise she learned from author Ken Keyes. Write down the name of a person who affects you at the top of a page. Draw a line down the center of that page, and write down all the things you like about the person on one side and all the things you dislike on the other side. Even if we dislike someone we can usually find something about that person that is okay. Your list might look like this:

MARTHA

Positive	*Negative*
good taste	lazy
passion for her work	sloppy
	emotional
	loud

Now write, before each item in the left column, "I love myself when . . ." *I love myself when I have good taste. I love myself when I have passion for my work.* Then write, before each item in the right column, "I don't like myself when . . ." *I don't like myself when I am lazy. I don't like myself when I am sloppy. I don't like myself when I am emotional. I don't like myself when I am loud.* This is a simple way to recognize that what you see in another person is really about you.

One day I got a call from my friend Laurie, who had taken my course. She was very upset. Laurie's former college roommate Christina was someone whom she'd admired for years. At the last minute, Christina had backed out of some plans she'd made with Laurie, and Laurie was aghast at her friend's behavior. She told me Christina was a spoiled, selfish, arrogant know-it-all. I gently reminded Laurie that when we're affected by someone's behavior it's a projection of our disowned qualities. Laurie insisted this had nothing to do with her. She was sure that Christina was finally showing her true colors. I asked Laurie to write down the things she did and didn't like about Christina. Here's her list:

CHRISTINA

Positive	*Negative*
leader	egocentric
elegant	selfish
spiritual	arrogant
successful	know-it-all
beautiful	uncaring

Laurie went through each positive trait and wrote, "I like myself when I am a leader, when I am elegant, when I am spiritual, when I am successful, when I am beautiful." Then she wrote, "I don't like myself when I am egocentric, when I am selfish, when I am arrogant, when I am a know-it-all, when I am uncaring." Laurie saw she was not owning the negative aspects of Christina, or the positive ones. Laurie had given Christina all her power by projecting onto Christina all the positive aspects that she wasn't connected to. When Christina disappointed Laurie, revealing her imperfections, Laurie felt cheated. When she found out that this perfect, spiritual, beautiful, elegant woman had flaws it underscored Laurie's flaws. Laurie had projected so much of her disowned self onto Christina that she felt lost and angry when Christina was being herself. In order to unplug, Laurie had to take back the parts of herself she'd projected onto Christina.

I told Laurie to try writing Christina a letter expressing her feelings. Even though she was never going to mail this letter, it was important that Laurie be able to express all the anger and resentment she was feeling. By the time she'd finished writing the letter, Laurie had decided she didn't want to give her power to Christina or anyone else. Laurie was ready to own her beauty, success, elegance, spirituality, and leadership qualities. One by one Laurie identified these aspects within herself. She reclaimed all her positive projections, and then her negatives. For Laurie, it was harder to own the positive than the negative. In fact, as soon as she embraced the positives she had no charge on the negatives. When we fully own something on one side of the scale, it often brings the opposite quality into balance. Christina turned out to be a catalyst for Laurie in finding her beauty and her light.

People come into our lives to help us restore our wholeness. The margin by which most of us judge ourselves is very narrow. If all the good is on one side and bad on the other, most of us will live in the middle, owning a small portion of our good and a small portion of our bad. We need to learn how to live in the full range of human capacity, and to not feel bad about doing it. Every emotion and impulse is perfectly human. We must fully embrace the dark in order to embrace the light. God, spirit, love: to me they are all the same. They are always there even if we cannot see them. They are waiting for us to invite them in. The doorway is in our hearts. When we're willing to open our hearts to all that exists, and start looking for the good rather than the bad in everything, we will see God. We will see love. Remembering we are the ones choosing what we see is essential. On some level, we ask for all the lessons we learn in this lifetime. Every incident, no matter how horrible, has a gift for you. And if you get your gift then I will get mine, for I am you and you are me in the world of the spirit.

EXERCISES

1. Take a few minutes and create a relaxed environment. Now close your eyes and take five slow, deep breaths. Imagine stepping into your internal elevator and go down

seven floors. When the door opens you'll be in your sacred garden. Walk towards your meditation seat while enjoying the beauty of your garden. Then ask yourself this question: What are the core beliefs that are running my life? Take a few minutes and then make a list of your core beliefs.

Then gently close your eyes and imagine the first statement on your list. Ask yourself the following questions. Take your time and listen for the answers coming from deep within.

a. Is this really my own idea, or did I adopt it?
b. Why do I have this belief?
c. Does this belief empower me?
d. What would I have to give up to alter this belief?

Take time to write in your journal when you have answered all the questions.

2. Write a short letter to each belief on your list, thanking it for serving you. Now invent a new belief to replace the old one. Make a verbal commitment to honor this new belief. Then open your eyes and write down the new empowering belief.

3. Write down a word you still cannot fully embrace or love. Close your eyes and find an early incident in your life that affected you in such a way that it made this quality offensive. Now, write down your interpretation of the incident. Underneath your interpretation write down five new interpretations of the event. Three positive ones and two negatives. If you can't think of any ask your friends or family. Thinking up new interpretations is a creative act that takes practice. Instead of being stuck with one interpretation try on many. You want to loosen the interpretation that has been causing you pain. Refer to page 122 if you have any questions.

CHAPTER 9

LETTING YOUR OWN LIGHT SHINE

Our deepest fear is not that we are inadequate. Our deepest fear is that we are powerful beyond measure," says Marianne Williamson in *A Return to Love*. "It is our light, not our darkness, that most frightens us. We ask ourselves, 'Who am I to be brilliant, gorgeous, talented, fabulous?' Actually who are you not to be? You are a child of God. Your playing small doesn't serve the world. There's nothing enlightened about shrinking so that other people won't feel insecure around you. You were born to manifest the glory of God that is within you. It's not just in some of us; it's in everyone. And as we let our own light shine, we unconsciously give other people permission to do the same. As we're liberated from our own fear, our presence automatically liberates others."

This chapter will show you how to let your entire light shine, how to embrace in yourself all the grace and magnificence you see in others. This means owning and embracing not just your dark shadow but your light shadow, too, everything positive that you've denied and projected onto others.

We live in a new age. It's a time of opening up and of healing and growth. It's not passive but it requires surrender—surrender of our egos and our old patterns. As Charles Dubois once said, "The important thing is to be able at any moment to sacrifice what you are for what you could become." The only thing that stops us from being our whole, authentic selves is fear. Our fear tells us that we can't fulfill our dreams. Our fear tells us not to take risks. It stops us from enjoying our richest treasures. Our fear keeps us living in the middle of the spectrum instead of embracing the full range. Fear keeps us numb. It blocks us from the exuberance and excitement of life. Fearful, we create situations in our lives to prove to ourselves that our self-imposed limitations are appropriate. To overcome our fear, we have to face it and replace it with love. Then we can embrace it. And once we can embrace our fear, we can choose not to be afraid anymore. Love allows us to cut that cord.

We fear our own magnitude because it challenges our core beliefs. It contradicts everything we've been told. Some of us recognize many of our gifts while others can see only a few, but it's rare that I meet someone who's comfortable with the full brilliance of their light. Everyone has different positive traits that he or she has difficulty embracing. Since most of us were told not to be cocky or conceited, we've buried some of our most precious gifts. These traits became our light shadow. We carry our light shadow around in the same bag with our dark shadow.

It's just as difficult to take back all the light aspects of ourselves as it is the dark ones. When I was in a drug detox center a woman came in to give a lecture to a group of us. She began by telling us that she'd graduated from college at the top of her class.

She had been married for thirteen years and had a fabulous relationship with her husband. She was a great mother and an excellent communicator. As she continued to tell us about all the things that she did well, I thought, "What a conceited bitch. Who does she think she is? Why do we have to listen to her?" Then she stopped, looked each of us in the eye, and said, "I came here to talk to you about self-love. About the importance of acknowledging all your good qualities and being able to share them with the people in your life." She explained that in order to love ourselves, we had to be willing to let our own light shine brightly. We had to acknowledge ourselves every day for all the good we've done. We had to take inventory of our lives and applaud our accomplishments. And when we let our light shine, we'd demonstrate to others that it was okay for them to shine too.

I sat in my chair in a state of shock. I sometimes bragged about my talents, but I never believed it was okay to appreciate and honor myself. My bragging came from insecurity, from my never really feeling good enough. The paradox of the situation was that, according to the lecturer, I didn't feel good about myself because I wasn't willing to own my God-given gifts. I wasn't willing to appreciate my talents. For some reason, I had always believed that downplaying the best parts of myself made me a better person.

That afternoon I learned one of the most valuable lessons of my life: not only is it okay to say nice things about ourselves, it's imperative. We must recognize our gifts and our talents. We must learn to appreciate and honor all that we do well. We must search out our uniqueness. Many people cannot own their success, happiness, health, beauty, and divinity. They are afraid to see that they are powerful, successful, sexy, and creative. Their fear keeps them from exploring these parts of themselves. But in order to authentically love ourselves we have to embrace all of who we are, not just the dark but the light as well. And learning to recognize our own talents allows us to appreciate and love everyone else's unique gifts.

Take a moment to quiet your mind. Take several slow, deep breaths and slowly read through the list below. After looking at every word, say to yourself, "I am _____," for every one. For example: I am healthy; I am beautiful; I am brilliant; I am talented; I am rich. Write down any word that you're uncomfortable with, on a sheet of paper. Include words that represent things that you admire in someone else but don't embrace in yourself.

Satisfied, secure, loved, inspiring, sensual, radiant, delicious, passionate, cheerful, joyful, sexy, forgiving, alive, fulfilled, energetic, confident, flexible, accepting, whole, healthy, talented, capable, wise, honored, holy, empowering, embracing, divine, powerful, free, funny, knowledgeable, affluent, enlightened, realized, balanced, brilliant, successful, worthy, open, compassionate, strong, creative, peaceful, fair, famous, disciplined, responsible, happy, pretty, desirable, blissful, enthusiastic, courageous, precious, fortunate, mature, artistic, vulnerable, radiant, conscious, faithful, magnificent, cosmic, attractive, complete, centered, cherished, romantic, warm-hearted, lucky, assertive, thankful, gentle, quiet, full, soft, wanted, extravagant, decisive, juicy, tender, willing, timely, irresistible, generous, beautiful, calm, carefree, easy going, patient, non-judgmental, cool, thoughtful, spiritual, loyal, connected, articulate, spontaneous, organized, reasonable, humorous, acknowledged, content, adored, playful, clean, fruitful, punctual, fun, understanding, self-assured, dedicated, optimistic, forward, intelligent, credible, active, glamorous, fearless, vivacious, warm, focused, innovative, nurturing, superstar, wonderful, leader, solid, champion, rich, choice-maker, simple, genuine, giving, assertive, adorned, prolific, productive, bold, sensitive

You possess all these qualities. All you have to do to manifest them is unconceal, own, and embrace each one. If you can see where in your life you have expressed a certain trait, or in what situations you can imagine yourself expressing a trait, you can own it. You must be willing to say, "I am that." The next step is to find the gift in that trait. Unlike our dark shadow, the gift is often obvious. But many of us have to face our own fear and resistance. Many of us have developed sophisticated defense mechanisms to reinforce our belief that we're not as talented or creative as someone else. And it's vitally important to be just as committed to embracing the positive as the negative.

It may be particularly tough to embrace certain traits that contradict external reality. It's difficult to embrace the word "rich" if you're out of work and in debt. In a case like this it's important to be able to imagine circumstances where you could become rich. A new job or career. If you cannot embrace a given word it's unlikely you will manifest the experience. When you look in the mirror and see an overweight person this can complicate things when the word you cannot embrace is "skinny." But if you don't own the skinny person within yourself, he or she will never be able to come out. If you're single and want to be married, you'll have to embrace your married aspect. For each of us, the things we resist will differ. Some of them will have lots of evidence to support your belief that they don't belong to you, but we can each find these aspects within us when we search with commitment.

Marlene was a woman in her early forties who attended my course. She was physically beautiful, but looked rather tired and sad. I went through the list of positive traits with the group and asked everyone to write down the words they couldn't embrace. Marlene had about twenty. We began with the same exercise we used for the negative traits, except this time Marlene sat in a chair while two people sat directly in front of her. Marlene began by saying, "I am successful" and the two other people mirrored back the word, saying, "You are successful."

During this exercise I watched Marlene own several traits. Then I looked at her list and told her to own the words "sexy" and "desirable." Marlene paused and shook her head. She said there wasn't a chance she could embrace those words. It turned out that Marlene was desperately trying to heal her relationship with her husband. Several months earlier she had discovered that he was having an affair and she was feeling very undesirable. When she finally started working on "sexy," at first she could hardly utter the word. Then, after a little coercing, she said, "I am sexy," but without any emotion. For about ten minutes she was just going through the motions. Marlene was sure sexy was not part of who she was, because she believed that if she were sexy, her husband wouldn't have cheated on her.

Marlene was doing this exercise with two women partners. I decided to ask a very attractive young man to change places with them. Marlene got very nervous when I told her that Tom was going to be her partner. When he pulled his chair up in front of Marlene and said, "You're sexy," she just sat there staring at him. Kneeling next to Marlene, I urged her to repeat the words back to Tom. With tears running down her face, Marlene finally said, "I am sexy." Tom looked Marlene right in the eye and said, "Yes, you are sexy." Marlene once again uttered, "I am sexy." They continued back and forth twenty times until Marlene could finally say, "I am sexy," without cringing or crying.

I then asked Tom to help Marlene embrace the word "desirable." Tom once again leaned forward in his chair and with utter certainty said, "Marlene, you are desirable." Marlene instantly started crying uncontrollably. No one, herself included, had told her that she was desirable for years. We worked with Marlene until she was ready to say "I am desirable." It started out as a mere whisper. Tom grabbed her hands, saying again, "You are desirable." Marlene joined in, repeating the words, "I am desirable," all the time feeling deep sadness about her relationship with her husband.

It took Marlene almost a half an hour before she could deal with the word desirable, but once she had said it out loud enough times she was able to evoke the memory of a time when she felt desirable. I could see in her face the moment she remembered that part of herself. Something lit up and reconnected her with that sacred part of her being. When she finally got it I asked her to stand up and scream, "I am desirable!" Marlene did it with joy in her eyes, and everyone applauded. We'd all been through an amazing process. It felt like we had given birth to a new person.

Feeling the pain of embracing certain things you've denied is essential to this process. Not all disowned aspects evoke such strong emotions, but when you find one that does, stay with it until you break the hold it has over you. The act of repeating a word over and over to yourself may bring a variety of responses. You might feel anger, resignation, fear, shame, guilt, joy, excitement, or any number of emotions. There is no right way to feel. But the important thing is to stay with it. No matter what you feel, don't run away, because by committing to the process of taking back the disowned parts of yourself, you're telling the universe you're ready to be whole.

Owning a positive trait that you've previously denied is scary, because it requires you to leave all your stories and excuses behind. You have to let go of all the reasons why you haven't gotten everything you've wanted in life. There was a woman named Patty in one of my courses who was unable to own "successful." She'd spent her entire adult life taking care of her husband and children. As a little girl, she'd been told to forget about her dream of playing the cello professionally. She was taught that a good woman got married and had children. Once or twice she'd mentioned to her husband that she would like to take cello lessons, but he'd always replied that it was a waste of money. Patty was now nearly sixty years old, with grown-up children on their own. And when she wrote down the names of people she admired, they were all successful women in the arts. When it was Patty's turn to do the mirroring exercise, she couldn't say, "I am successful." She was somewhere between laughing and crying.

Patty had decided that success meant having a career. But when I asked Patty if she had been a successful mother, she said yes, all her children were doing well. Then I asked if she had a successful marriage and Patty smiled, answering yes, she'd been married more than thirty years. I asked Patty if she had ever made a successful meal and she laughed and said she was a pretty good cook. Slowly, Patty began to see she was successful. It took Patty nearly twenty minutes to say the word, but eventually she owned it. She left the course walking tall. Ten months later I got a letter from Patty saying she'd started playing the cello again at a little theater near her home when they needed her. She said that having embraced her success she now felt confident enough to manifest more of her desires.

We are taught not to acknowledge our greatness. Most of us believe we possess some positive traits but not others. But we are all things: those that make us laugh as well as those that make us cry. We are every beautiful and ugly trait rolled into one. It is time to manifest all of your qualities. When you can own your entire list you will truly be in the presence of God.

Harry was a seventy-five-year-old man who had been in a recovery program for codependency for almost ten years. He came with his wife to my course to see if he could heal their troubled relationship. The moment I met Harry he told me how emotionally sick he was. He had been in a twelve-step program so he was comfortable affirming his unhealthy emotional state. We began owning positive traits and when I saw Harry's list there were two words that were missing: healthy and whole. Harry didn't believe it was possible for him to be emotionally healthy. So I gave him an exercise. For the rest of the day every time he wanted to say he was sick he had to say he was healthy and whole.

I could tell Harry was having trouble digesting these qualities. In the middle of the day, when we began mirroring positive traits, Harry, with deep resignation, started to say, "I am healthy." He was able to embrace that word and move on to, "I am whole." We were all moved by Harry's courage and determination. He told us during the middle of the exercise that he finally got it, and that this was the first time he ever remembered embracing the healthy, whole part of himself. The day continued to open up for Harry when we did a forgiveness exercise with the group. After owning all his positive and negative qualities, Harry was able to unplug from the negative projections he had made on his wife. This allowed Harry to see Charlotte as a strong, beautiful, loving woman who cared for him deeply, instead of an unhealthy woman in a codependent relationship. Harry and Charlotte then were able to do the exercise together, and they had a tremendous healing. They both expressed a great deal that they'd been withholding. By embracing their own light they were able to embrace each other's.

Soon after the seminar, Harry had a stroke and died. His wife called to thank me for my work with her husband. Charlotte told me that a profound healing had taken place within Harry when he embraced all of himself. He had allowed his marriage to be strong and exciting for the first time in years. Charlotte also said that Harry knew he was going to die, and from reading the journal Harry had kept during the course, she knew that he died at peace, loving and accepting his total self. He saw divinity not just in himself but in his wife. Charlotte wept tears of joy that they had the opportunity to experience each other's beauty before Harry left this earth.

Once we take back our positive projections we experience inner peace—the deep peace that lets us know we are perfect exactly the way we are. Peace comes when we stop pretending to be something other than our true selves. Many of us don't even realize we are pretending to be lesser people than we really are. Somehow we have convinced ourselves that who we are is not enough. Allow the world within to manifest itself and it will show you the road to freedom—freedom to be sexy, desirable, talented, healthy, and successful.

When you don't recognize your full potential you don't allow the universe to give you your divine gifts. Your soul yearns to realize its full potential. Only you can allow this to happen. You can choose to open your heart and embrace all of yourself, or you can choose to live with the illusion of who you are today. And forgiveness is the most important step on this path to self-love. We must see ourselves with the innocence of a child, and accept our misdeeds and misgivings with love and compassion. We have to set aside our harsh judgments and come to terms with the mistakes we've made. We must know that we're worthy of forgiveness. This divine gift teaches us that part of being human is making mistakes. Forgiveness comes from the heart, not the ego. Forgiveness is a choice. At any moment in time we can give up our resentments and judgments and choose to forgive ourselves and others. When we take back all our projections and find our gifts, we're able to find compassion for ourselves. It then becomes natural to have compassion for those whom we have resented. When we see in ourselves what we've hated in others, we can take responsibility for what exists between ourselves and them.

Rilke wrote that "perhaps all the dragons of our lives are princesses who are only waiting to see us once, beautiful and brave. Perhaps everything terrible is in its deepest being something that needs our love." Love which does not include total acceptance of you is incomplete. Most of us are trained to look outside ourselves for the love we need. But when we let go of our need for love from the external world the only way to comfort ourselves is to go within, to find what we strive to get from others and give it to ourselves. We all deserve it. We must allow the universe within, our divine mother and father, to love us and nourish us.

When my friend Amy was going through her divorce and trying to heal her relationship with her husband, she couldn't seem to shake loose of her anger. Every day something would come up that would leave her upset. Amy was desperately trying to love herself through this emotional process, but it often seemed impossible. Finally, in an attempt to clear her negative feelings, Amy wrote out a list of all the things she loved and hated about Ed. Of course, this was quite a long list on both sides, but slowly Amy was able to take back her positive projections, as well as most of her negative ones.

Yet again and again one word kept coming up that Amy couldn't own. The word was "dead." When Amy was angry she saw Ed as emotionally dead. She tried embracing herself as dead but she couldn't see how she was like him. Amy had all the evidence in the world to prove how emotionally alive she was. Amy could easily laugh, scream, and cry. She experienced the entire spectrum of emotions. But nevertheless the word that affected her was "dead." So she continued her search to find the dead part of herself.

Months passed. Amy's divorce was final, and she was fine. But whenever she got upset, there was that word again—dead. Then Amy started dating Charles, who was much younger than she. One day she and her son, Bobby, were going on an outing with Charles. When Charles got in the car, he popped out the Sesame Street tape that they always listened to and put in Aaron Neville. He started singing and turning around to laugh with Bobby, who was shining bright at all the excitement. Suddenly tears started pouring down Amy's cheeks. She couldn't stop. It was such a beautiful moment; she didn't know why she was so upset. Then Amy realized she was feeling dead. Here was Charles, young, full of energy, excited about life, and she realized a part of her was dead. A part of her had stopped jumping around, singing and dancing.

The good news was that after she embraced this dead part of herself, Ed no longer plugged her in. By loving and nourishing this disowned aspect, Amy was able to forgive both Ed and herself. It was her anger with Ed that had led her on this treasure hunt to find this hidden part of herself. Without it Amy wouldn't have discovered this part of herself that needed to be awakened. By embracing her deadness she was able to reclaim her aliveness.

Search around for stored-up anger. If you are fearful about discovering your anger, remember that your power is buried along with it. Anger is only a negative emotion when it is suppressed or dealt with in an unhealthy way. When you have compassion for yourself you can easily allow all aspects of yourself, your love and your anger, to coexist within you. Whenever I'm judging myself or others, I know I'm holding onto negative interpretations of a quality or an event. It is essential at times like this to let myself express my emotions in a healthy way.

A woman named Carla came into one of my courses with a big smile on her face and a beautiful glow surrounding her. Carla worked hard during our weekend workshop, but when it came time to do anger work she froze. Carla said she had no anger. We were working on an exercise that involved hitting pillows with a plastic bat. Exercises like batting usually release a lot of blocked energy. Carla, a large woman and about forty pounds overweight, should have been able to clobber those little pillows, but she could hardly find the strength to raise the bat over her head.

After the session I went for a walk with Carla and casually started to talk about the power of anger. I suggested that our anger often holds the key to opening our hearts, and when released it allows all our vital life energy to flow through us. Still, Carla couldn't admit she was holding in any anger. I asked her why she had so much trouble losing her unwanted fat. She told me it was a temporary problem. I suggested that Carla do anger release work for thirty days even if she didn't feel angry. I told her that if she just batted pillows every day for five or ten minutes it could unleash some amazing things that were buried inside of her. When Carla asked me what she should think about while batting I suggested if she really couldn't find anything that made her mad she should just bat the fat.

Months went by before I spoke to Carla again. When she finally called me she was still having trouble losing weight, making money, and finding the intimate relationship she desired. My first question was about the anger-release work I had suggested. She told me she wasn't doing it because "I'm not angry at myself or anyone else." I told her that if we don't have everything we desire it's because we're withholding it from ourselves—we feel we aren't worthy. When we feel unworthy, it's often because we think there's something bad about us. And when we feel there's something fundamentally bad about us we usually feel angry. Carla still insisted she had no resentments towards herself or others.

An entire year went by before Carla called back. Her first words were, "Guess what? I'm hostile!" I shouted with joy! Carla had found her hidden qualities. She said she'd felt stuck the entire year. Nothing in her life had been going well. Finally, in a crunch for money, Carla had taken a roommate into her home. After about a week, she started feeling angry and hostile towards this woman. No matter how she tried to hide these feelings, every time her roommate walked into her home Carla felt upset. She decided she'd made a big mistake, and told the woman she would have to move out. Not having anywhere to go, the woman told Carla she would move out when she found another place to live. Carla was beside herself and asked the woman to move immediately. She found herself doing what she called "evil things" to get rid of her. Finally Carla threatened the woman, telling her if she didn't move within three days she would throw all her belongings out on the lawn.

Carla's deeply hidden dark side finally showed its face, and she could no longer deny these shadow aspects of herself. Carla was able to see her anger, own it, and embrace it. She told me it was so shocking at first that she didn't know what to do. So she used the tools she'd learned in the course and went within herself to find the gift of Hostile Harriet. In response to the question "What is your gift to me?" Hostile Harriet said her gift was life energy. She told Carla if she would love and honor her she would give her all the energy she needed to fulfill her dreams. Carla was able to pick up the bat that had lain unused in her house for over a year and whack her pillows till the stuffing came out. She told me how good it felt to let out all that anger and rage. Months later Carla felt better than she had in years. She had accepted another aspect of herself and forgiven herself for her angry feelings. Her business tripled and she started an exercise and diet plan to rid herself of her unwanted weight.

It often takes time before we're able to see certain aspects of ourselves. Even when we have all the knowledge and tools to embrace all of our selves, there will be times when we aren't ready to see something painful about ourselves. The truth is that the healing you're looking for in your relationships will not come from another person. It must come from you first. It will come from communion with all the qualities that live within you.

Desperation comes from the gulf between God and self. To remember we are one with all is to reawaken the God within us. Our divinity and our passion are intertwined. When we awaken our passion we awaken our divinity. We have learned that passion is intended for external things, other people, other places, other things. It's time to unleash your passion for yourself. And finding love for all of who you are is a complex task. It should be easy and natural, but for most of us it's the most difficult job we will ever encounter. If you've been working for a long time and haven't been able to fully love and embrace all of who you are, don't be discouraged. This is our biggest assignment. It is the assignment we were sent here to fulfill.

At this point I suggest creating rituals for yourself if you're serious about doing the work of nurturing yourself. When I tell people to go home and nurture themselves they often look puzzled. They always ask, "How do I do that?" It is different for everyone but the most important thing is to have the *intention* of nurturing yourself. Once you have the intention, you can work on the specifics.

Start by taking a baby picture of yourself and putting it up in a place where you'll see it a couple of times a day. If you go to an office every day put another one there. This baby is an aspect of you, which if cared for will bring you all the joy and happiness you ever desired. You might look a little different from the self in that photo, but you're still a beautiful being. Our hearts open up to love when we see babies. We project all our love and innocence onto them. When my son was born, it amazed me that strangers came up to me everywhere I went. They told me how beautiful my baby was, how sweet he was, how healthy he looked, how special he was. None of these people had ever seen him or me before, and yet all of them were sure that he had these particular traits. They projected some aspect of themselves onto him and shared it with me. My son could have been a nightmare, but no one would have noticed.

Consider what you project onto babies. Do you think about their beauty, their innocence, their perfection, or their sweetness? Do you think they're spoiled, out of control, selfish, or rotten? Do you think they have bad parents who don't know how to care for them? Whatever your thoughts, remember that they're all aspects of you that you're projecting. Unless you've spent time with a child and can give an objective evaluation, you're probably seeing some aspect of yourself in them.

Putting up a baby picture often makes people think about the innocence within them. Most of us have more compassion for babies than we do for other adults or for ourselves. If a baby knocked over a glass of water near your computer, would you look at him or her with disgust or would you see the innocence of a child and just clean the water up? We judge babies less. Think of yourself as an innocent child who only needs your love, care, and approval. Allow this child to receive that love. Imagine yourself giving love to this child every day. Close your eyes and let an image of yourself when you were young come to the front of your mind. Ask, "What can I do for this child today? How can he or she feel loved and nurtured?" Listen to your inner voice. Hear what this being within you wants and needs. They might need to hear you say, "I love you, I accept you," or "I appreciate you." They might want a night off from your busy schedule, a trip to the movies, or an afternoon nap. Most often people seem to need rest and appreciation. We're so busy being busy that we've forgotten how to take care of ourselves.

Morning is a sacred time for all of us to connect with our divinity. As the stillness of night gives way to a new day, the thoughts and feelings of the morning can set the foundation for our entire day. Taking just a few minutes in the morning for yourself before you start rushing around sets the stage for a wonderful day.

Try giving yourself an oil massage before your shower, and thank God for all the parts of your body. Starting with your head, rub in the oil and thank God for your features, your senses, your voice, ears, and brain; then work down to your beautiful neck and shoulders, into your arms and hands, and through your chest and stomach. Thank your body for being there for you, for housing your soul, and for being a strong foundation. Move into your buttocks and then down your legs, making sure you focus your attention on every part of your body that you are massaging. When you get to your feet remember that they've carried you around for many years so take the time to bless them and appreciate them. With your eyes closed, scan your entire body and feel whether there is any place where you feel stress or uneasiness. Bring your loving attention to these areas: thank them for communicating with you and let the tension leave your body now.

If you don't have time for the oil massage, you can use a variation while taking your shower. Wash each part of your body with love, and acknowledge that area for doing its job and supporting the rest of your body. This whole process doesn't have to take more than five minutes. If you have more time, then spend more time. The important thing is to honor yourself. Give yourself the message that you are important. Honor and respect your genius. By authentically honoring and respecting yourself, you'll be able to do the same for others, drawing like-minded people and positive situations into your life.

You could also take time every night to do something special for yourself. A bath is a great way to relax and unwind from the day. Lighting candles, turning down the lights, and sinking into a tub full of warm water is a wonderful way to nurture yourself. You can meditate, just be silent, or listen to music that feeds your soul. If you don't like baths, you could try setting up a nurturing environment for yourself every night before you go to bed. Lighting candles, using aromatherapy or incense to enliven your mood—these are all great ways to end your day. Turn on music or meditate in silence but allow the nurturing ambiance you design to penetrate your whole being.

When I first started my own healing process I made a list of all the things I could do for myself. It took me a while to figure out that going to the gym was not nurturing my soul. It did have a purpose, which was to make me look better and stay healthier, and it was good for my ego, but it didn't nurture my spirit. It's important to distinguish between what's good for your self respect and what's good for your soul.

I had just broken up with a man at the time and was feeling

quite lonely. Instead of sinking into my sadness I decided to take on the project of falling in love with myself. Every night I'd make myself a beautiful dinner, even though I didn't really know how to cook very well. When I went to the store I'd ask myself, "What could I eat tonight that would nourish me?" While I was eating I'd listen to music and light incense. After dinner I'd make a fire for myself and light candles all over my house. It was mood setting just for me. After a week or two, I couldn't wait to go home and be with myself. Instead of waiting to find someone to romance me, I romanced myself—and it worked.

This nighttime ritual changed everything in my life. Every day I woke up feeling content, relaxed, and good about myself. Every day I learned more about nurturing my soul. Do for yourself what you would like someone to do for you. If you like flowers, buy yourself flowers. Play soft music, light candles. Go to a store and find some aromas that you like and start using them every day. Become important to yourself. Getting dressed for dinner even if you're dining alone can be a nurturing experience if you don't often pay attention to your appearance. Put on clothes that make you feel good even if you're not going out. Treat yourself like royalty. You are!

The world mirrors yourself back to you. If you love, nourish, and appreciate yourself internally it will show up in your external life. If you want more love, give more love to yourself. If you want acceptance, accept yourself. I promise that if you love and respect yourself from the deepest place of your being, you will call forth that same level of love and respect from the universe. If you think you are doing this and your external world does not look like you think it should, I ask you to look inside one more time. Uncover the lie. Uncover what you are not allowing yourself to have, what you most desire.

EXERCISES

1. This exercise is designed to identify and release toxic emotional energy. Our focus will be on forgiveness. Our intention is to release any emotion that's blocking you— anger, resentment, regret, or guilt—feelings that stop you from forgiving yourself or someone else.

   Journaling is a good tool to help process your emotions. It encourages whatever comes into your mind to flow out onto the paper. It allows the emotional toxicity in our bodies and minds to express itself freely. Once we can grant this toxicity being and allow it to exist without judgment it will be released.

   Start by clearing off anything on your lap or in your way. All you need to have close by is your journal and a pen. You might want to put on some soft music, and light some candles or incense to help you relax. Now close your eyes. Use your breath to quiet your mind and surrender to the process. Take five slow, deep breaths.

   With your eyes closed, imagine being in an elevator and push the button that will take you to the fifth floor. As the door opens, you see that you are in a beautiful garden. As you gaze out at the greenery and the flowers, you see a nice chair, a perfect place for you to sit and relax. As you sit down comfortably in this chair, take another slow, deep breath. Now ask yourself the following questions and allow the answers to come to you. Then open your eyes and write them down. Repeat this process for each of the four questions, making sure to close your eyes and take a few slow, deep breaths so you can clear your mind and hear the answers from your heart.

a. What story have I created about who I really am that explains my current life circumstances?

Journal

b. What resentments, old wounds, anger, or regrets do I carry in my heart?

Journal

c. Who in my life have I been unwilling to forgive?

Journal

d. What needs to happen for me to forgive myself and others?

Journal

e. Now make a list of people you need to forgive and write a short letter to them. If your list is long, write as many letters as you can. What you don't finish now you can complete later.

f. What do you need to say to yourself to be current with your life up to now?

2. *Write a forgiveness letter to yourself.* Make a list of the three people you admire the most. Write down three qualities that inspire you about each of them. Then make a master list of the nine qualities. Go through the list of

positive traits on pages 139–40 and write down any that you cannot embrace within yourself. Add these words to your list of nine positive qualities.

Now, bring this list of words and go sit or stand in front of a mirror. Taking each word individually, look into your own eyes, and repeat the following sentence: "I am (a) _____." Continue to repeat the sentence until you no longer feel any resistance to the word. Choose a time each day to own one or two words from your list. If you get stuck and are unwilling or unable to own a particular word, move on and come back to it later.

CHAPTER 10

A LIFE WORTH LIVING

Manifesting your dreams begins with the difficult task of discovering what they truly are. As children, we follow the footsteps of our parents and teachers. Most of us accept their guidance and wisdom about what classes to take in school. They influence our choice of hobbies, sports, and clubs that fill up our free time. As we get older we often choose our careers and our mates based on ideals established by our elders. But at what point do we stop listening to these external voices and tune in to our inner guides? When do we decide that perhaps the path we're on is not really our own? Could this be the reason we feel something is missing in our lives?

These are the kinds of questions we fear most because they require us to second-guess what we've been taught. Have you ever questioned your belief in God? For some, to question holy doctrine is a mortal sin. But if we don't challenge our most basic beliefs we won't grow as spiritual beings. Our lives will simply run along lines established by our parents, and we'll never go beyond those boundaries that were set when we were kids. This chapter is about stepping out into unknown territory. It will guide you towards manifesting a life of greatness and serenity. Instead of saying, "I can't do that," you need to ask, "Why shouldn't I do that? What am I afraid of?" That question challenges the ties that bind you. This chapter is dedicated to finding your life's purpose.

Questioning whether you're on the right path may sound easy. The difficult part is hearing the answer from the heart. Your head will have one response, but your heart may have another. Fear may urge you to maintain your current direction, yet love may urge you to take a turn. You must quiet your mind to hear your highest calling. You must open your heart to find where love resides. If you choose to follow your passions and desires, then you must be still enough to hear the answers from your soul. Walk out only as far as you can stand with your head above water and the scenery will always look the same. Dare to venture into deeper waters and a magical world awaits you.

But we're afraid to drown. Afraid to be wrong. Afraid to fail. Are your desires important enough to make you willing to face your fears? Do you want it bad enough? The choice is yours. You can choose to change your attitude from resignation to commitment, from a state of fear to a state of love. The first step is to question yourself, to literally change your internal statements to questions. Change "I am a failure" to "Could I be a success?" Change "I am bored with my life" to "Could I be exhilarated?" Change "My life doesn't make a difference" to "Could I make a difference in the world?"

Our need to be right, to feel safe, stands in our way of this commitment to life. We feel unsafe if we question our motives. Would you rather be right about being powerless or be wrong about your ability to be great? Would you rather be in control of a small sum of money or unsure about how to balance a large bank account? Would you prefer to stay in a job you dislike or risk creating a business you love? Are you happy? Are you following your heart's desires? If you knew you only had one year to live would you be doing what you are doing now? Would you make the same choices for your life?

Close your eyes and focus on a place deep inside where you feel safe and comfortable. Ask yourself what you'd like to be doing right now in your life. Ask why you're not pursuing that dream. What are you afraid of? Ask yourself the question I just posed you: what you would do if you only had one year to live? What would you change? Holding the answers in the stillness of your heart, make the commitment to alter your life so that you may manifest your dreams. Make the commitment to always listen and hear your own truth. Make the commitment to let the universe guide you toward your heart's desire. Just making these commitments will change your life. By doing so you are telling yourself and the universe, "I am worthy of having what I desire and I am going to do what it takes to fulfill my desire." W. H. Murray wrote:

> Until one is committed there is hesitancy, the chance to draw back, always ineffectiveness. Concerning all acts of initiative (and creation), there is one elementary truth, the ignorance of which kills countless ideas and splendid plans: that the moment one definitely commits oneself, then Providence moves too. All sorts of things occur to help one that would never otherwise have occurred. A whole stream of events issues from the decision, raising in one's favor all manner of unforeseen incidents and meetings and material assistance, which no man could have dreamt would come his way. Whatever you can do, or you can dream, begin it. Boldness has genius, power, and magic in it.

Without commitment the universe cannot bring forth the events we need to realize our desires.

Unfortunately, most of us don't commit to what we really desire. We lie in bed at night and pray for a better life, a better body, a better job, but nothing changes. This is because we are lying to ourselves. What we pray for and what we have committed to are often totally different things. We pray for a healthy lifestyle but we are committed to being sedentary. We pray for a rewarding relationship but we are committed to sitting at home. We are most comfortable with the status quo. But when we realize that no one is coming to save us, or do it for us, and that our old wounds are there whether we love them or hate them, then we realize that we're the ones who have to fulfill our potential. It's easier to blame others than to take responsibility. "What if I fail? What if it hurts? What will others think of me?"

I first got off of drugs a couple weeks before my twenty-ninth birthday. I had chosen the path of drug-induced intoxication for almost fifteen years. My life was full of pain and depression. On the outside I looked like I had it all together, but inside I was dying.

After being released from my fourth treatment center, I finally made a commitment to heal my life. Before this moment whenever I felt a little bad or a little angry or a little lonely I would head right back down the road that was taking me nowhere. But on this one beautiful Miami day, I was driving down the street in my convertible feeling the breeze across my face. I was completely in the present moment, full of gratitude for being alive and being straight.

A vision came to me that I could really heal myself from all my addictions: cigarettes, drugs, food, shopping, and men. I saw myself going around the country, sharing my message of health. I heard myself saying "You can do it, you can have it all, you can heal yourself completely!" My body trembled with emotion. I felt exhilarated and scared at the same time. I felt an overwhelming need to give back all the love and support that had been given to me. At that moment, sitting at a stop light in front of the Aventura Mall in North Miami Beach, I knew that my life could and would make a difference. I knew that if I made a commitment to do whatever it took to work through all my anger, rage, stubbornness, righteousness, to confront my ego and all its grandiosity, I knew that I, Deborah Sue Ford, could give something to this world.

This is the vision that brought me to this point in my life. Whenever I wanted to stop, give up working on my emotional life, a little voice within me would say, "No. You're not finished. You're not healed." Every time I wanted to point my finger and blame another human being, a small voice within would ask, "What is your role in this drama? Why are you bringing this into your life?" Every cell in my body was aligned with my commitment to heal completely. So whenever I didn't want to go to therapy or attend a seminar or deal with the next layer of my pain I did it anyway, because I was more committed to healing than I was to feeling good all the time.

I went to Overeaters Anonymous meetings, not because I was overweight but because I found myself eating entire chocolate cakes in a sitting. I had taken drugs to change the way I felt, and I began to see how I might easily do the same with food. Because of my commitment, I chose not to substitute one addiction for another. I could have just eaten myself into oblivion, but I chose to deal with the issue. I knew that to truly change my life I was going to have to be uncomfortable for a while. This commitment to heal was the catalyst for my transformation. Without it I would have continued to numb my pain with addictive behaviors.

I want you to know that I'm far from what you might consider perfect. But it's no longer my mission to be perfect. My mission now is to be whole, to be complete, to be perfect and imperfect at the same time. My mission now is to listen to my inner wisdom and to live my life as fully as possible. My commitment now is to love myself as much as humanly possible, for I know that when I do I will in return be able to love you. The processes I share with you are the ones that ended my suffering and gave me the knowledge and the courage to heal myself completely. If I hadn't lived from this core commitment, I wouldn't be writing this book right now. This commitment led me to explore hundreds of different healing modalities. This commitment intuitively guided me to people, places, and experiences that taught me the lessons I needed.

Don't be afraid if you don't know what you want. Simply make a commitment to live up to your full potential. Live in the moment, and the universe will show you your unique gifts. Your commitment will guide you to the places you need to go, the books you need to read, and the people who will assist and teach you. There's an old Buddhist saying, "When the student is ready the teacher will appear." I've had hundreds of teachers appear in my life over the last fourteen years. They've shown up in the form of girlfriends, lovers, and business partners. Some of them have shown up as thieves and liars. Everyone that I have formed a relationship with—positive or negative—has come into my life to teach me, guide me, and help fulfill my commitment. My friend Annimika says, "Everyone who comes to your door is coming to heal you." Even the people who come to my seminars are there to heal me. Understanding this has changed every interaction I have with other people.

I have a friend who is at least a hundred pounds overweight.

He constantly tells me how well he eats and that his diet is not the problem. In a sense he's right. Food is not the problem. The problem is that he lies to himself about his eating habits. He is a food addict and is unwilling to acknowledge it and go for help. Addiction is powerful. Denial is a killer. It kills people's chances of achieving their goals. When we make a commitment we have to be willing to dig at the roots of our current situations. If you're really committed to losing weight, then discovering you're a food addict is a blessing—it's a necessary step in the process of achieving your goal. But if your first commitment is to believing that you don't have an eating disorder or that you just have a poor metabolism, it will be very difficult to achieve your secondary desire to lose weight. Dig deep enough to find the true cause of your problem, make your commitment, and your dreams will come true.

Be a warrior when it comes to manifesting your dreams. So many people I've met talk about their passions as if they were treasured coins, locked in museum cases. They pray silently late at night for their dreams to come true, but their fears and resignation make them passive. Do you know who gets that coin? It's the person who makes a plan of action, the person who writes a mission statement. The person who commits. This is the road to a more enlightened life, to living the truth.

My friend John is a thirty-six-year-old songwriter and singer with extraordinary musical talent. When I first started talking to John about his musical gifts he wouldn't even listen to me. He would say, "Please, stop, I don't want to think about it." It took a long time before John admitted he had fantasized about winning a Grammy and performing his music in front of millions of people. But after a while, whenever John spoke about his music and his dreams his entire face began to light up. When he played his songs his passion radiated from deep within him. It was so clear that John's music was his heart's desire, and as he began to see it himself, he needed only to manifest it.

One evening I sat down with John and we looked at what underlying commitments he had that would stop him from becoming a best-selling singer and songwriter. We took a sheet of paper and on one side articulated his commitment to becoming a famous singer-songwriter, and on the other side we wrote out all his beliefs that would stop him from fulfilling this dream. Here's what it looked like:

Underlying commitments
I, John Palmer, can't do this because I'm not talented enough.
It's not a realistic goal.
It's not what a good Italian boy would do.
I didn't study enough when I was taking piano lessons.
I just spent the last five years trying something similar and
    didn't make it, so why would I make it at this?
I'm just a kid and I'm not ready to face it.
I don't have time for unrealistic dreams. I have to get a real job.

All these underlying commitments and beliefs had kept John from ever seriously considering his music as a career. As an outsider I couldn't imagine why John couldn't see his talent the way I experienced it. But when we gave a voice to all of his fears, it was easy to see why John never pursued a career in the music industry. John was unconsciously more committed to the obstacles than he was to discovering if his vision had any validity.

We have to unconceal all the beliefs that keep us from attaining our dreams. I call these underlying commitments because they are agreements we have made with ourselves to not reach our true goals. Whether you decide to go after your dreams or not, it's important to question what's driving you, as well as what gets in the way of your heart's desires. If we don't ask these questions, we'll continue to sell our lives short. Whether your goal is to diet, to make more money, or to have a better relationship, you need to go back and discover your underlying commitments and beliefs. You don't need to suppress these beliefs. You need to allow them to exist, so you can choose ones which empower you and leave the rest behind.

Take a moment now and pull out a piece of paper. Write down a goal that you haven't been able to fulfill. Write down all your beliefs and underlying commitments that relate to that goal. Write them quickly, without trying to think too hard, and they'll just flow out of you. Then go back and question each one. Is this belief a fact or a judgment? This is a vitally important question. When we went through John's list it looked like this:

Underlying commitments

JUDGMENT: I, John Palmer, can't do this because I'm not talented enough.

JUDGMENT: It's not a realistic goal.

JUDGMENT: It's not what a good Italian boy would do.

JUDGMENT: I didn't study enough when I was taking piano lessons.

JUDGMENT: I just spent the last five years doing something similar and didn't make it at that. Why would I make it at this?

JUDGMENT: I'm just a kid and I'm not ready to face it.

JUDGMENT: I don't have time for unrealistic dreams. I have to get a real job.

Everything in John's way was a judgment, either his own or that of a friend or family member. And these judgments were running John's life. Unfortunately, most of us are in the same situation. We allow our internal beliefs to control our lives. It's interesting to discover that our friends and family can usually be found repeating the same beliefs that we've adopted. They convince us, or we convince them that these judgments are true. I was recently at a party with several of John's friends. When I brought up the subject of his music three different people repeated to me, almost word for word, why John couldn't make it in the music business. Did John get his limiting judgments from his friends, or did he talk them into believing his own judgments? Either way, John was not making a commitment to his true desires.

The decision to alter your life is serious. After years of working with people, I've discovered that many people like to talk about change but are unwilling to let go of behaviors that keep them stuck in negative patterns. Ask yourself if your search for peace, happiness, and wholeness is an ongoing drama, or if you're ready to take control and be the one that shapes your experiences. No one out there can fix you. But you can fix yourself. You are the one with the power, the answers, and the ability to change your life. And you are the only one.

We spend billions of dollars each year trying to change our bodies, our health, and our relationships, yet most of us are still dissatisfied with some area of our lives. We're in a constant state of wanting something we can't seem to reach. This state of wanting, of dreams that never get fulfilled, is the result of pretending we are on our way to somewhere when really we are stalled. How can you have a true desire or a true goal without a plan to achieve the goal? Without the commitment to do whatever it takes to fulfill your goal, it most likely will never come to fruition. Psychologists call this magical thinking. We fool ourselves into thinking we will someday achieve our dreams without ever taking any practical steps. Some people meditate on their desires. Others talk to their friends, visit gurus, or go to church. Some people spend their money on psychics and fortune tellers. And some live vicariously through television and movies while their dreams stay on hold.

All these are simply ways to avoid facing the truth. Prayer without action is not prayer. It's dreaming. How can God help us if we won't help ourselves? I once heard a story of a man who had a deep faith in God. He was often heard telling his friends that his chaotic life would work itself out because God would take care of him. One day a huge storm caused serious flooding in the town where this man lived. While other members of the community packed their belongings and fled, the man stayed put, believing that God would take care of him. The water began to seep under his doors and through the windows. A fire truck drove by and rescue workers yelled to the man, "Come on, you can't stay here!" "No," he said to them, "God will take care of me!"

Soon the water was waist-high, the streets turned to rivers. A Coast Guard boat came past the man's house. The crew yelled out to him, "Swim out and come on board!" "No," the man yelled back. "God will take care of me." The rain kept pouring down until the man's entire house was flooded. Then a helicopter flew over his house and the pilot spotted the man praying on his roof. Lowering the ladder, the pilot got on the loud speaker, "You, down there, grab hold of the ladder and we'll take you to safety!" Again, the man proclaimed his conviction: "God will take care of me." Finally, the man drowned. At the pearly gates of heaven, the man had never felt more betrayed. "My God," he said, "I put my faith in you and prayed to you for my rescue. You told me you would always take care of me, yet when I needed you most, you were not there." "What do you mean?" replied God. "I sent you a fire truck, a boat, and a helicopter. What more do you want?"

There is nothing wrong with faith. There is nothing wrong with affirmations. But at some point *you* must take the next step. Make a commitment to have what you want in life and then make a plan to *get it*. It's there waiting for you but most likely it won't fall into your lap. If you want to know whether you're serious about changing something in your life, ask yourself if you have a plan of action. If the answer is no, go back and see if you're really committed to achieving your goal. A plan of action ought to be written down on paper. If it's only in your mind it may be more of a dream than a plan. Plans in our minds tend to get lost or forgotten, or pushed aside by everyday life. Tell yourself you'll have more of a chance of achieving your goal if you have it written down and keep it at hand.

Without a plan our desires tease us and leave us feeling empty. Gandhi once said, "I have not the shadow of a doubt that any man or woman can achieve what I have, if he or she would make the same effort and cultivate the same hope and faith. What is faith worth if it is not translated into action?" Most of the suffering I see in people is the result of their not fulfilling their dreams. They spend their days thinking about being in the wrong relationship or not having the right job, and when I ask how they plan to change these aspects of their lives they look at me like I'm kidding. They believe that when they finally "fix themselves" they will easily manifest all their desires. Question this belief.

Making a plan of action is easy. The most difficult part of doing the entire process is taking the time to do it. I suggest you pick one goal that you have been trying to achieve—the goal that seems the least daunting. Then break it down into four parts. A daily plan, a weekly plan, a monthly plan, and a yearly plan. Ask yourself: What can I do on a daily basis to fulfill my goal? What can I do on a weekly basis to fulfill my goal and continue to monthly and yearly? Make a calendar with different projects that will bring you closer to achieving your desired result. When you finish your plan you have set out on the path to truly realizing your dreams.

Recently I worked with a man named Nick who wanted me to figure out why he couldn't reach the next level of success in his business. He kept telling me that he felt there was something holding him back from really making it to the top. After many hours of conversation I asked him how much money his company brought in on a yearly basis. He told me it was between six and seven million dollars. Shocked, I asked him why he wasn't happy with this large amount of money. Nick's answer was that if only he could generate another four million dollars a year in revenue, he wouldn't have to work so hard. When I asked how much money he made from the six or seven million dollars, Nick said he barely met his payroll. I suggested that maybe this wasn't about bringing in more money, but about cutting down his overhead so he could see 30 percent profit from this six or seven million dollars. Nick didn't like what I had to say. He had already decided the only way to really make it big was to bring in more business.

The cosmic joke was that Nick was a business consultant who advised businesses on how to make money. After much discussion Nick mentioned that his father had told him some twenty years earlier that Nick would never make any money and that he'd always spend more than he made. Nick clearly believed his father, and had made an unconscious commitment to honor his father's words. Now Nick needed to make a new commitment to himself. To be successful he needed to make a 30 percent profit on the revenue he brought in no matter what. Once he made this commitment, Nick started seeing dozens of places where he could cut his overhead but to enact them Nick had to confront many issues in his business, which were difficult to deal with. He had always liked being the kind of boss who never checked anyone's expenses and didn't have to adjust anyone's salary when things got tough. He loved playing the big shot and had tricked himself into believing that meant he was a successful businessman.

So Nick called a meeting with all the top people in his firm and told them he needed their help making the business profitable. He asked them how they could cut the company's expenses with an eye to making a 30 percent profit. For the first time, Nick allowed all the people in his business to really contribute their opinions. Nick literally had to reinvent himself as a businessman to achieve his goal. He had to take responsibility for the condition of the company and for his ineffective management techniques. It was not an easy process. After a great deal of suffering, Nick realized his commitment to having a huge successful business was coming from his head and not his heart. In the process of reorganizing his business, he started questioning whether he really wanted to live in Central America where he'd gone many years ago to start his company. He also began to question whether he really wanted to keep traveling around the world twenty days a month. Once Nick allowed himself to question his business life, he discovered he was more dissatisfied with his personal life than he had originally thought.

But because Nick made a commitment to overcome the obstacles to his satisfaction and happiness, the universe brought many events into his life that broke down the walls. These events led Nick to discover that his first commitment was not his heart's desire. Nick was open and ready to receive this information and has now found a new path for his life that fills his soul with peace. He has realized that he never wanted a huge business with lots of employees. He has realized that what he wanted was a wife and a family, and that in order to have that he needed to stay in one place. Nick has made a deeper commitment to his spiritual growth and to forming lasting friendships, which are now vital to his personal fulfillment.

Like many of us, Nick had to go through a lot of pain to discover his heart's desire. If you have a commitment to alter an area of your life and are not meeting your objective, look at what underlying commitments you are fulfilling instead. You must be willing to discover that some of your desires may be coming from your head and not your heart. Your head will trick you into believing that you want more, better, and different expressions of what you already have. We have to expose these ego-driven desires for what they are, and replace them with desires of the heart.

Go beyond the clamor of your intellect. Like Nick, most of us think that fulfilling the mind's desires will fill our emptiness. But only when we follow our deeper calling will we find lasting fulfillment. What will bring satisfaction and balance to your life? Who are you in this life and what are you meant to bring to this planet? Most of us have only glimpsed what our souls yearn to express in this life. But many of us have chosen to ignore our calling. Others of us are still waiting, hoping, praying for our chance to express our unique gifts—not realizing that the only moment that exists is now.

Keeping your word is essential to your plan for change. What you say to yourself and others does count. If you tell yourself that you are going to eat healthier foods and don't do it you are broadcasting to yourself and the universe that you can't be trusted. If you say you're going to get a new job next year and don't do it, you're sending a message that you can't be counted on. Even if it's a small task, like balancing your checkbook, if you don't do it, you're saying to yourself and to the universe that you don't keep your word. These broken promises wear down our self-esteem.

Years ago, I went to a program called the Forum, a three-day personal growth and development seminar. It was there that I learned the value of keeping my word, and as a result my whole life changed. It's very simple. Do what you say. If you're not going to do it, don't say you are. Have your *word* be the most important asset you have. Treat it like gold. If you treat it like gold it will bring you gold, you will be able to create what you want in the world. Each time you do what you say you're going to do, you're training yourself and the universe that you can be counted on. Then when you start to work on larger goals, when you say I am going to make more money, fall in love, write a book, or open a clinic, you will be able to do it.

When we constantly lie to ourselves it's difficult for us to believe in ourselves. The New Year's resolutions you never follow through on are just wishes. Your word, if not taken seriously, is nothing but noise. Communication is a great gift but your words have a much greater gift to give you. They can assist you in designing your life. They can give you power and freedom. When you make a commitment to do something for yourself or someone else, and you know you can follow through, you have power. When you want to change something in your life or achieve a goal and you know you're capable of doing it, you have freedom.

In *The Soul's Code,* James Hillman says, "You are born with a character, it is given, a gift as the old stories say, from the guardians upon your birth." Discovering the gift you were born with, your life's purpose, is a process. It takes time and a peeling away of the layers that conceal what is rightly yours, your unique imprint. Each one of us has a calling. You have something no one else on this planet has. Your calling might be to heal people, teach people, nurture people, or to discover a cure for cancer. It might be the way you interact with people, it might be an expression of creativity, or it could be raising children. No matter what your purpose, if you commit to finding and fulfilling it, it will fill up your heart and leave you feeling inspired.

Dr. David Simon says:

The concept of *dharma*, or purpose, holds that there are no spare parts in the universe. Each of us enters the world with a unique perspective and set of talents, which enables us to unfold an aspect of natural intelligence that has never been expressed before. When we are living in dharma, we are in service to ourselves and to those affected by our choices. We know we are in dharma when we cannot think of anything else we would rather be doing with our life. One of the greatest services we can perform for another person is supporting them in the discovery of their dharma. This is one of the most important roles that parents play in their children's lives.

Don't panic if you do not know what your dharma or purpose is right now; just begin to do this work and trust the answers you hear from within. Your internal voices are there to guide you to fulfillment. People often ignore their intuition and their inner guides for so long they silence the part of them that can help them the most. When you know you should be doing one thing and you constantly do another, you're killing your spirit and denying your essence. This makes it difficult to discover your vision. At some point, most of us have seen at least a glimmer of our calling, but for whatever reason we have chosen not to follow it. Now when we think we are ready to see it and live it, it eludes us. You must listen to the part of yourself that has been trying to guide you to your higher purpose. Ask this aspect to reawaken and guide you to do your best. Ask your inner guides to show you your life purpose, and they will. You must unveil your personal calling and remember there is a reason for you to be alive.

When I first got off drugs, I worked in the retail clothing business. The more work I did on myself the more I sensed that I needed to find something new to do with my life. Completely bewildered about what that was, I got on my hands and knees every morning and said the prayer that I learned from the book of Alcoholics Anonymous.

God, I offer myself to Thee—to build with me and do with me as Thou wilt. Relieve me of the bondage of self, that I may better do Thy will. Take away my difficulties, that victory over them may bear witness to those I would help of Thy power, Thy love, and Thy way of life. May I do Thy will always!

The ritual of a daily prayer gave me the belief that one day I'd discover my life's purpose. So when I saw my vision, months later sitting in my car, I knew it was Spirit showing me my path.

Many people deny their calling for fear that they will not reach it. They choose not to see their gift rather than face what looks like an unachievable future. Many people have resigned themselves to never finding their unique gift. But discovering our life's purpose is truly something to strive for. It is our birthright. Our minds set our only limitations.

I suggest you create a personal mission statement. Write down five to ten words that really inspire you. Then use the words to write a powerful statement that will guide you and keep you on the track of fulfilling your soul's purpose. The first time I tried this was in "The Advanced Course" offered by Landmark Education. When it was my turn to share my vision for my life, I had no ideas. Then without thinking this came out of my mouth: "I am the possibility that all people can invent themselves from nothing." At first I didn't know what I meant. But after some thought, I saw that I truly believed we can each be anything our hearts desire. I also believe that no matter where you've been or what you've been through, you're capable of reinventing yourself over and over again. I believe you do not have to stay stuck in old patterns or old behaviors. You can change friends and professions as many times as necessary until you are in a place that expresses your unique imprint.

This mission statement that I created reminds me daily of what I am here to do. It calls on me to become the best I can be and leaves me open to reinventing and expressing a new self as often as I wish. Find a statement that has personal meaning to you. No one else needs to understand or even know your statement. Use it to remind you where you are going and keep you in the present moment.

Gandhi said, "The only devils in the world are those running around in our hearts. That is where the battle should be fought." Shadow work is about opening your heart and making peace with your internal devils. It is about embracing your fears and weaknesses and finding compassion for your humanity. Give yourself the gift of your heart. As soon as you open your heart to yourself you will open your heart to all others.

You are lovable. You are deserving. You are enough. Trust your inner wisdom and trust that at your core there is goodness. Go beyond your self-imposed limits and make a commitment to living a life you love. Ask the universe for love and support. Ask God to fill you with compassion and strength. Face where you are at this moment and then move to higher ground. Grant yourself permission to have it all, you deserve it!

EXERCISES

1. In this exercise I'd like you to create a mission statement for yourself in the form of a power statement. This power statement should be an affirmation of who you want to be in the future. You could focus on your health, relationships, career, spiritual growth, or all of the above.

   Close your eyes and step into your internal elevator. Take a few slow, deep breaths and allow yourself to relax completely. When you open your eyes you'll be in your sacred garden. Walk slowly to your meditation seat. When you feel quiet inside, call forth an image of your sacred self. Allow this image to become strong, vivid, and bright. Ask your sacred self to come forward and bring you a message that will give you all the strength and courage you need to live the life of your dreams. If you have trouble and cannot hear your message, make one up that empowers you. Allow words to come to your awareness that make you feel strong. When you are finished thank your sacred self for assisting you and easily come back into external awareness. Take out your journal and write down everything you saw in your visualization.

   This statement will empower you to go to the next level of personal growth in all areas of your life. I suggest that your statement be as short and simple as possible. Hopefully, you will use it daily as a way to remind yourself of your highest vision for your life. Below are a few examples of power statements that people have created.

a. I am a spiritual being worthy of honesty, love, and abundance.
b. The universe is my friend and lover always meeting my needs.
c. Wherever I look I see beauty, truth, and possibility.
d. I am wise and all knowing and I allow the universe to fulfill my desires.
e. There is no genuine desire I cannot manifest today.

You want to create a statement that lights you up and excites you when you repeat it. This is a statement meant to empower you in your everyday life. It could be as simple as, *"Who I am makes a difference."*

It takes time to form new habits, so make a commitment to repeat this statement to yourself for the next twenty-eight days no matter what happens. Try repeating it as soon as you wake up in the morning, before you even get out of bed. If that's not possible, do it right before bed at night. It's great to start and end your day by remembering your highest commitment to yourself. I recommend you write out your power statement on Post-it notes and put them up all over your home, office, and car. The more you bring it into your awareness, the more meaningful this statement will become. Make it visible and accessible until it's deeply ingrained in your consciousness.

2. Another powerful process to call forth your future is sometimes called *treasure mapping,* creating a collage to visualize your dreams. This is great to do with a group of friends. All you need is a piece of poster board, a few of your favorite magazines, a pair of scissors, and some glue.

Treasure Mapping Visualization

Close your eyes, return to your elevator, and go down seven floors. When you step out of the elevator you'll see your beautiful garden. Walk through your garden and notice the flowers and trees. Look at the lush green leaves and smell the essences of all the lovely flowers. It is a beautiful day and the birds are singing. Notice the color of the sky. What is the temperature of the air? Is it cool or warm? Do you feel a breeze across your face? Inhale the beauty and the scents of your sacred garden. Now go to your meditation chair. Sit comfortably; allow yourself to relax. Now picture your life a year from now. You have everything you ever desired. All your dreams have come true; you are peaceful and content. You trust yourself and the universe. Your search for meaning is complete and you feel confident about your future. What does your life look like? Spend some time imagining it. What are your relationships like? How is your health? What are you doing for fun? How is your family? How are your finances? What are you doing for spiritual growth? Now go five years into the future. What do your relationships look like now? How is your health? What are you doing for fun? How is your family? What do your finances look like? What are you doing for your spiritual growth?

After you've done the visualization, go through your magazines and cut out pictures that excite you. Don't think during this process; just go through the magazines as fast as you can and pull out pictures that have positive energy for you. Set a timer for ten or fifteen minutes. If you take more time than this, you'll start to second-guess yourself. Simply be guided by your first impulses. When you have your supplies ready, go ahead and begin.

When you've finished your collage, put it up in a place where you can easily see it. Use the images to remind yourself of your heart's desires.

3. Now see how your present life compares to what you saw in the visualization. Take out a sheet of paper and write down everything in your life that is inconsistent with the future you saw in the visualization and in your collage. Then write down everything you are doing to create the future you imagined. If you are not taking the necessary steps to create your future you can change that by acknowledging the truth and making a plan of action. The most important issue here is telling yourself the truth. The things in your life that are inconsistent with the future you desire should be noted, then you can begin to make a plan to eliminate them from your life.

Once again, we consider whether this is all worthwhile, whether it's worth your time and energy to restore yourself to wholeness, to shift your thoughts from hopelessness to enlightenment. When you discover that what lies beneath the surface of your consciousness are simply unprocessed thoughts and feelings, your pain can be healed. When you allow all the parts of yourself that you've repressed to come to the surface, you can exhale with relief. You can breathe easy again. When you peel off the mask that hides your vulnerability and your humanity, you'll come face to face with your true self.

I've guided you through a long, deep process in order for you to discover that who you are at the deepest level is "enough." We've explored the world of the holographic universe where we're all created equal and where everything is perfectly balanced. We discovered the amazing world of projection where the universe so generously mirrors back all our disowned aspects. We learned to see that not only do we possess all the qualities we most abhor, but that these negative traits possess positive gifts. They are there to guide us to where our hearts long to go, to a place where compassion lives. By owning and embracing what we most fear and hate, we're able to bring ourselves back into balance. As Deepak Chopra says, "Non-judgment creates silence of the mind." A silent mind is clear to hear the words of our greatest good, words from Spirit.

We all have the opportunity to clean out our castles. To open the doors to every room. We can step inside and clear out the dust that hides the brilliance and beauty of each room. We can see that each room calls for something different in order to shine bright. Some of our rooms need love and acceptance. Some need revamping. Others just want attention. No matter what thing each room needs, we know that we are able to give it. If we want to live to our full magnitude, we have to allow all parts of our magnificent selves to stand and be respected. We must step out of our bubble of false perceptions and stand in a wave of new clarity. As individuals, we have to expand our internal consciousness to include every part of our humanity. If you saw yourself as a small house, you have to create the internal space necessary to hold an entire castle.

Do you really want inner peace? If you do, it's yours. Surrender. Stop fighting. Stop defending. Stop pretending. Stop denying. Stop lying to yourself. Own up to your defenses, your walls, to the cage that surrounds you. Don't strive for perfection, because it's the desire for perfection that leads us to build these walls. Strive for wholeness, and for light and dark to live equally. Just as every thing has a light side and a dark side, so does every person, because to be human is to be it all.

I heard a great story told by Guru Mayi, the leader of the Siddha Yoga Foundation. The ruler of a prosperous kingdom sends for one of his messengers. When he arrives the King tells him to go out and find the worst thing in the entire world, and bring it back within a few days. The messenger departs, and returns days later, empty-handed. Puzzled, the King asks, "What have you discovered? I don't see anything." The messenger says, "Right here, Your Majesty," and sticks out his tongue. Bewildered, the King asks the young man to explain. The messenger says, "My tongue is the worst thing in the world. My tongue can do many horrible things. My tongue speaks evil and tells lies. I can overindulge with my tongue which leaves me feeling tired and sick, and I can say things that hurt other people. My tongue is the worst thing in the world." Pleased, the King then commands the messenger to go out and find him the best thing in the entire world.

The messenger leaves hurriedly, and once again he comes back days later with nothing in his hands. "Where is it?" the King shouts out. Again, the messenger sticks out his tongue. "Show me," the King says. "How can it be?" The messenger replies, "My tongue is the best thing in the world, my tongue is a messenger of love. Only with my tongue can I express the overwhelming beauty of poetry. My tongue teaches me refinement in tastes and guides me to choose foods that will nourish my body. My tongue is the best thing in the world because it allows me to chant the name of God." The King is well satisfied, and he appoints the messenger to become foremost among his personal advisors.

We all have the tendency to see things as black and white. But there is good and bad, and dark and light in everything. To deny it anywhere is to deny it everywhere. There is nothing we can see that is not God, and when we can see that in ourselves then we are able to see it in everyone.

Our deepest longing is for peace, love, and harmony. Our life is a brief, precious journey, and our mandate is the expression of our unique gifts. To express our individuality is to reclaim our divinity. It's easy to lose sight of that which is most precious. Don't withhold your love or your forgiveness. Don't hide your compassion or your grace. Our most important relationship is with ourselves, our whole being, including our shadow. It's important to remember that all good relationships are continuous. We need to continually grow and overcome obstacles that get in our way. Good relationships challenge us to become more than we may think we are. They compel us to stretch ourselves, to expand our hearts. We must become intimate with our shadow selves; they are a holy and sacred part of each of us. You need only commit to staying in the process of seeing yourself, of loving yourself, and the process of opening your heart. Appreciate your divinity and you will appreciate the gift of life. In this state you'll begin to immerse yourself in the wonderful, mystical experience of being human.

To reach Debbie Ford directly, please call or write to her at:

P.O. Box 8064
La Jolla, CA 92038
(619) 699-8999

e-mail: www.fordsisters.com

Debbie Ford conducts seminars on the dark side at the Chopra Center for Well Being in La Jolla, California, where she is a consultant, teacher, and integral faculty member. She also leads her own day and weekend Shadow Process workshop nationwide. She lives in La Jolla with her son, Beau.